FAMOUS FLORIDA RECIPES

300 years of good eating

By Lowis Carlton

Illustrations by Joseph Brown, Jr.

A Great Outdoors Book

Great Outdoors Publishing Company
An Imprint of Finney Company

ISBN 10: 0-8200-0810-9
ISBN 13: 978-0-8200-0810-3

Photo credits:
> Lowis Carlton: page 51
> Florida State News Bureau (Florida Dept. of Commerce):
> > pages 41, 45, 79, 95
> United Fresh Fruit and Vegetable Association:
> > pages 16, 31, 61, 90

Great Outdoors Publishing Company
An Imprint of Finney Company
8075 215th Street West
Lakeville, Minnesota 55044
www.floridabooks.com

Printed in the United States of America

Contents

About the Author

Lowis Carlton has written for a variety of national publications and is also the author of the book *Florida Seafood Cookery*. She was graduated magna cum laude from the University of Miami with a B.A. and M.A. in English, and was named to Phi Kappa Phi. She also holds a B.S. in Home Economics from Florida International University, where she concentrated on work with the chefs in the school's highly-rated hotel school.

While serving as food editor for the *Miami Herald*, Lowis won the Vespa Award, a national newspaper award for food writing. She has served as a judge for the Pillsbury Bake-Off and has traveled extensively in Europe studying food customs.

Lowis was gourmet editor for *Palm Beach Life* magazine for many years, and was also a columnist for the Florida Department of Agriculture, writing about Florida products for 200 newspapers throughout the U.S.

After residing in Miami for many years, Lowis and her husband moved to St. Lucie West, Florida. Though husband Claud is semi-retired, Lowis maintains a full schedule developing and testing recipes, participating in church functions and writing Florida fiction. Hobbies for the Carltons are world travel, bridge, fishing and enjoying the recipes contained in this book and others in her extensive cookbook collection.

Foreword

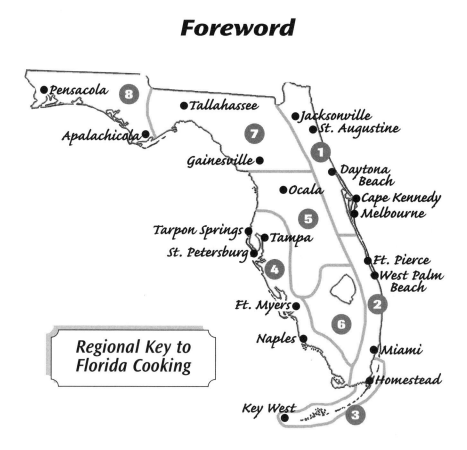

Pensacola 8
Tallahassee
Apalachicola
Gainesville
Jacksonville
St. Augustine
7
1
Daytona Beach
Ocala
Cape Kennedy
Melbourne
5
Tarpon Springs
St. Petersburg
Tampa
4
Ft. Pierce
West Palm Beach
2
Ft. Myers
6
Naples
Miami
Homestead
Key West
3

Regional Key to Florida Cooking

No one way with food can qualify as the single definitive Florida cuisine. Down through history, Florida has experienced a steady influx of people from various areas of the world.

They found in Florida bountiful supplies of fish, fruits and vegetables, as well as home-grown beef, pork and wild game. Each group, using traditional recipes from their homeland, melded Florida products into those recipes to create a cuisine both unique and varied.

For example, you could find:

— in Key West, a British family from the Bahamas, dipping into a pot of conch chowder…

— an aristocratic woman whose family came to Tallahassee from Virginia before the Civil War, serving a ladies' group ambrosia, pound cake and tea…

— a Seminole Indian girl on the Brighton reservation cooking a pot of turtle stew over an open fire...

— a Cuban refugee cook in Miami mixing a batch of peppery guacamole made from avocados.

Floridians, all of them, practicing genuine Florida cuisine! And all so different.

For some 300 years, Florida cuisine has developed and expanded as new residents arrived. And it is still changing, taking on the spice and kick of food prepared by transplanted Puerto Ricans and Mexicans, as well as French-inspired dishes of former Louisiana Creoles; the simple sturdy fare of New Englanders; and the Wiener Schnitzel of brides coming from Germany after World War II to make homes for their G.I. husbands.

In Florida homes, food runs the gamut from down home to elegant gourmet fare. From these homes as well as many excellent restaurants comes this collection of the most prized recipes of the Sunshine State.

Cook and enjoy!

1 *Historic Northeast Florida*

*Gates of old St. Augustine, the oldest
continuously settled U.S. city, founded in 1565.*

A picturesque lighthouse stands as a stately sentinel at Amelia Island along the coast of North Florida where American history really began.

In April 1513, Ponce de Leon sailed into the harbor of yet-to-be-named St. Augustine. He was amazed and delighted at the wealth of sub-tropical flowers and foliage in this land of sunshine and blue skies. But he set sail, seeking a non-existent Fountain of Youth.

Spain sent her top-ranked admiral in 1565 to seize the harbor and all land from Labrador to Mexico. Later, the Spaniards built a string of forts from Cape Florida to Santa Elena, with St. Augustine's coquina rock structure, Castillo de San Marcos, as the headquarters.

New culture arrived with a band of Minorcans late in the 1700s. These quiet, industrious people established civilized customs and higher standards of food. Dr. Andrew Turnbull brought them from the Mediterranean island, and descendants of the original groups still cook the traditional dishes.

It was not until July 10, 1821, that the Stars and Stripes fluttered over the fort, after secession of Florida from Spain. The embattled little community fought through the Seminole Indian Wars, then became a "state of the American nation" in 1845.

Throughout the Seminole War from 1835 to 1842, national newspapers reported such news as how Indians were tricked into capture under a flag of truce, and the escape of Osceola's men from the dungeon in the fort. They told of the Indian leader's seizure and imprisonment while he was on his way to confer with American leaders seven miles from St. Augustine. His death in Fort Moultrie, S.C. caused much bitterness, for public sentiment was with the Seminoles, but things calmed down when the Indian War finally ended.

The town was in Union hands from 1862 to the end of the War Between the States. There was a long slumberous period until 1874, when the first locomotive arrived and tourists began coming.

Henry M. Flagler, enchanted with the quaint air of the drowsy little Spanish town, started the renaissance of St. Augustine in 1885, with construction of the Hotel Ponce de Leon. Thus St. Augustine was launched as a winter resort. Flagler extended a railroad southward and made the city headquarters for the Florida East Coast Railway and Hotel System.

The city has never lost its atmosphere of ages past, with its horse-drawn carriages, the old fort, coquina rock houses with Spanish balconies, and the fanciful combination of Spanish, Minorcan and Southern food.

Seasonings were—and still are—spicy, heavy on thyme, tomatoes and onions, and a fiery hot pepper called Datil, believed brought to America by the Turnbull colonists, whose descendants now live in New Smyrna.

Pilau was so much in favor in time past that when it couldn't be made with chicken, pork, ham or shrimp, it was filled with speckled butter beans for a meatless main dish.

Other early-day recipes for clam chowder, boiled mullet and yellow rice have remained popular. At Easter, there were traditional recipes used to make treats given to street singers who serenaded the families—some sweet foods, some hot. Two favorites are Fromajardis, cheese-stuffed baked pastries, and Minorcan crispees, baked pastry circles sprinkled with cinnamon sugar.

South of St. Augustine is the lively city of Daytona Beach, famous for its 23 mile-long beach of pure white, hard-packed sand. Built along the Atlantic on the Halifax River, the city began with establishment of Spanish missions late in the 16th century. Many Indians were converted to Christianity before the English conquered the area in 1702. British plantation owners were succeeded by Spanish until finally, in the 19th century, Georgia colonists built sugar plantations and stayed permanently.

The town was named Daytona in 1870 by Mathias Day, and the word Beach was added in 1924. Pine, palmetto and cabbage palm thrive outside the city and in the spring, orange and grapefruit blossoms from citrus groves perfume the air.

Follow the St. Johns River—the nation's longest *north*-flowing river—to arrive in Jacksonville, a busy seaport that is one of the state's major cities.

It was near the mouth of the St. Johns River that Jean Ribault and a party of French Huguenot explorers anchored on April 30, 1562, marking the discovery of the river by the Europeans. Ribault marked the place a French possession and was followed in 1564 by 250 French Huguenot colonists.

At the foot of the hill now called St. Johns Bluff, they planted their colony and called it Fort Caroline. After Ponce de Leon claimed all Florida for Spain, Pedro Menendez was sent to wipe out the settlement, which he did. He returned in triumph to his camp, where he established the town of St. Augustine.

Because it was a good place to ford the river, the Indians called Jacksonville, Wacca Pilatka, translated into English as Cowford. The English developed the Indian Trail from below St. Augustine to the Cowford, then to Georgia into the "King's Highway."

In 1816, Lewis Zachariah Hogans became Jacksonville's first settler, and a few frame cabins were built. Late in June, 1822, the town was surveyed and named in honor of General Andrew Jackson. At the end of the Seminole War in 1842, the city began its climb to its modern status as a leader among Florida cities. Today, it is one of Florida's major cultural, financial, industrial, transportation and commercial centers. Downtown development includes The Riverwalk, a landscaped, two-mile complex of pavilions, restaurants, shops and marina on the banks of the St. Johns River. The downtown also boasts a Skyway Express people mover.

Just one of the numerous bridges spanning rivers and waterways is the award-winning Napoleon B. Broward bridge soaring over the St. Johns River, with towers reaching 472 feet.

This north Florida city retains an old-time Southern charm, with palatial homes, lushly landscaped parks and—everywhere you look— enormous oak-draped oaks and pines.

Home port for a big shrimp fleet is Mayport on Jacksonville Beach. Along with traditional Southern fare, seafood and fish such as grouper, snapper and dolphin are popular, especially on backyard barbecue grills as well as restaurant menus.

MINORCAN AND OLD ST. AUGUSTINE RECIPES

Fromajardis Cheese Cakes

These Minorcan cakes play an important part in a popular St. Augustine tra-dition. On Easter Eve, the Fromajardis folk song was sung by strolling men singers in serenade to a house. If these cheese cakes and wine were served in abundance by the household, the singers sent their praises, then went to sit on the seawall and enjoy the refreshments. If no cakes were forthcoming, the singers did not hesi-tate to sing out their criticism of the stingy man, to the delight of the neighbors.

For days before Easter, women were busy baking, preparing not less than half a flour barrel of the cheese cakes. In the spring of 1843, William Cullen Bryant heard the singers during a St. Augustine visit. He wrote the Mahonese dialect version of their song in his "Letters of a Traveller."

Pie Dough:
2 cups all-purpose flour
1 tsp. salt
$1/8$ tsp. nutmeg

$2/3$ cup chilled Crisco shortening
2 Tbsp. chilled butter
4 Tbsp. water

Filling:
$1/2$ lb. aged Cheddar cheese
4 eggs, well beaten
$1/8$ tsp. salt

$1/4$ tsp. cayenne pepper (or less, to
  taste)
4 Tbsp. melted butter

In a bowl, sift together flour, salt and nutmeg. In a second bowl, place the shortening and butter. Cut half of the shortening and butter into the flour mix-ture with a pastry blender or two knives, blending until it resembles cornmeal. Add the remaining shortening and butter and blend until the mixture forms pea-sized balls. Sprinkle it with water and blend lightly until dough gathers into a smooth ball. Place dough in waxed paper and chill it in the refrigerator while preparing the filling.

Grate cheese; beat in eggs, salt and pepper. Roll chilled dough thin. Cut in five-inch rounds. On a half of each round, cut a cross. Place one tablespoon of cheese on uncut half of dough circle. Fold to make a half circle; pinch edges together. Brush with melted butter. Bake in 375°F oven 20 minutes or until golden brown. Cheese will puff up through the cross. Makes about 15. Serve with Florida orange wine.

Peach Jam Cake

1 cup white raisins, soaked in peach
    brandy
1 cup butter or margarine
2 cups sugar
3 eggs, separated
1 cup peach jam
3 1/2 cups flour

1 1/2 tsp. baking powder
1/2 tsp. salt
1 tsp. each cinnamon, nutmeg, allspice
    and ginger
1 cup buttermilk
1 tsp. baking soda
1 cup chopped pecans

Place raisins in brandy and let stand overnight. Cream butter and sugar until light. Add egg yolks; mix well. Add jam and beat until smooth. Sift together twice the flour, salt, baking powder and spices. Stir baking soda into buttermilk and add to creamed mixture alternately with the flour, stirring to blend well each time. Toss nuts and raisins in a little flour; fold into cake mixture. Beat egg whites until stiff and fold in. Pour into oiled tube pan and bake at 350°F for 45 minutes or until cake tests done.

Stove-Top Chicken Pilau
(Pronounced "Chicken Pur-lo")

4 slices bacon
1 Tbsp. green pepper, chopped
1 onion, chopped
1 28-oz. can tomatoes
1 cup okra, thinly sliced or half of one
    10-oz. pkg. frozen cut okra, thawed
1 Tbsp. sugar

1 tsp. salt
1 cup water
1/4 tsp. ground red pepper
1 small hot green pepper, chopped
1 cup long grain rice
2 cups cooked chicken, cut in cubes
1 Tbsp. chopped parsley

Fry bacon in skillet until crisp. Set aside to drain on paper towel. In bacon drippings, saute onion and green pepper until tender. Add canned tomatoes, okra, sugar, salt, water, red pepper, hot green pepper, uncooked rice and chicken. Cover tightly; simmer until rice is cooked, about 25 minutes. Serve in a colorful bowl, topped with crumbled bacon and parsley. (Note: This recipe is peppery. It is wise to start with half the quantities given for the ground red pepper and hot green pepper and adjust the amounts to suit your taste.) Serves 6.

Minorcan Christmas Candy

3 cups freshly grated coconut
2 cups sugar

1/2 cup coconut milk
3 Tbsp. white Karo syrup

Stir coconut, sugar and milk to blend well; add syrup. Over very low heat, cook, stirring constantly until mixture becomes thick and heavy. Drop in small teaspoonfuls onto waxed paper and allow to harden. (Note: if prepared coconut is used, soak 1/4 cup coconut in warm milk for one hour, then strain it to get coconut milk.) Makes about 60 candies.

NORTHEAST FLORIDA SPECIALTIES

Scallops St. Augustine

$1/2$ lb. scallops, fresh or frozen
2 Tbsp. margarine or butter
1 Tbsp. olive oil
1 tsp. marjoram
$1/2$ tsp. salt
$1/4$ tsp. white pepper

1 cup sliced mushrooms
2 Tbsp. sliced green onion
$1/2$ cup sherry wine
$1/4$ cup white wine
2 Tbsp. cornstarch
2 servings cooked, seasoned wild rice

Thaw scallops if frozen. Rinse scallops to remove any remaining shell particles; cut large scallops in half. Melt margarine with oil in 10-inch frying pan over medium high heat. Add scallops, marjoram, salt and pepper. Cook 2 to 3 minutes until scallops begin to turn opaque. Remove from pan with slotted spoon and set aside. In the same pan, cook mushrooms and onions 3 to 4 minutes. Add sherry and white wine; cook until volume is reduced by $1/2$. Add cornstarch and cook until thickened, stirring continuously. Reduce heat, replace scallops in pan and cook 3 minutes longer or until scallops are done. Serve immediately over hot cooked wild rice. Serves 2.

Lemon-Baked Chicken with Spiced Peaches

1 3-lb. broiler-fryer chicken, quartered
1 Tbsp. flour
1 tsp. Accent
$1/2$ tsp. salt

$1/8$ tsp. pepper
$1/2$ tsp. paprika
1 Tbsp. butter or margarine
3 Tbsp. lemon or lime juice

Place chicken in shallow baking dish. Combine flour, Accent, salt, pepper, paprika; sprinkle over chicken. Dot with butter. Bake uncovered at 375°F for 30 minutes. Sprinkle with lemon juice; bake 20 minutes longer. (Only 200 calories per serving!) Serve with spiced peaches.

Spiced peaches:

1 29-oz. can cling peach halves
1 tsp. whole cloves

$1/3$ cup brown sugar
$1/4$ cup lemon or lime juice

Drain peach syrup into saucepan. Stud peach halves with half the cloves; set aside. Bring syrup and remaining cloves to a boil; boil rapidly until reduced to $1/2$ cup. Add sugar, lemon juice and peaches; bring to a boil. Remove from heat. Serve warm with chicken. Serves 4.

Southern Barbecued Chicken

3 dressed young broilers, split
2 Tbsp. catsup
2 Tbsp. vinegar
1/2 tsp. dry mustard
1 Tbsp. lemon or lime juice

1/4 tsp. Tabasco sauce
2 Tbsp. Worcestershire sauce
2 Tbsp. water
5 Tbsp. melted butter
1/2 tsp. paprika

Rub each broiler half with salt, pepper, melted butter. Place on broiler rack, skin face down, and cook under moderate heat until brown and almost tender. Turn and cook other side. Mix ingredients and use to baste chicken frequently during broiling. Serves 6.

Barbecued Shrimp

2 lbs. raw shrimp
1/3 cup minced onion
3 Tbsp. olive oil
1 cup catsup
1/3 cup lemon juice
2 Tbsp. brown sugar

1/2 cup hot water
2 tsp. prepared mustard
2 Tbsp. Worcestershire sauce
1/4 tsp. salt
1 tsp. chili sauce

In heavy pan, saute onion in olive oil until transparent. Peel and devein shrimp. Add all remaining ingredients except shrimp to onion in pan. Turn heat to low; cover and simmer 10 minutes. Place shrimp on broiling platter; cover with sauce. With shrimp 6 inches below broiler, broil about 6 minutes or until shrimp are cooked. Turn once. Serve hot with remaining sauce. Serves 4.

Roast Pork, Spanish Style

6 lb. pork loin roast
2 cloves garlic
1 tsp. salt

1/4 tsp. pepper
4 Tbsp. oregano
2/3 cup fresh lime juice

Cut garlic into slivers; make slits all over the roast and insert garlic. Combine salt, pepper and oregano. Rub this over the meat. Place fat side up on a rack pan in preheated 450°F oven; immediately reduce heat to 350°F and cook uncovered 30–35 minutes per pound. If a meat thermometer is used, it should read 185°F. When pork begins to brown, baste frequently with lime juice. (This roast has slight garlic flavor with a crisp, tart crust.) Serve with spiced crabapples. Serves 8–10.

FLORIDA VEGETABLES

Red-and-White Tomato Molded Salad

1 envelope gelatin
1/2 cup cold tomato juice
1 1/4 cups hot tomato juice

1/2 tsp. salt
1 Tbsp. lemon juice
egg salad layer (below)

Soften gelatin in 2 tablespoons cold tomato juice. Stir in remaining cold, then hot tomato juice. When dissolved, mix in salt and lemon juice. Pour into oiled loaf pan; refrigerate until almost firm; add egg salad layer. Chill until set; unmold and serve with mayonnaise mixed with mashed avocado. Serves 8.

Egg salad layer:
1 envelope gelatin
1/2 cup cold water
1 tsp. salt
2 Tbsp. lemon juice
1/2 tsp. Worcestershire sauce
1/8 tsp. pepper
1/4 cup pimiento, finely chopped

4 hard-cooked eggs, chopped
2 tsp. onion, grated
1/2 cup celery, finely chopped
1/4 cup green pepper, finely chopped
1 Tbsp. celery seed
3/4 cup mayonnaise

Soften gelatin in cold water. Place in top of double boiler and heat until dissolved, stirring slowly. Add salt, lemon juice, Worcestershire and pepper. Cool. Add mayonnaise and remaining ingredients, stirring until well blended.

Broccoli Soufflé with Cheese Sauce

4 Tbsp. butter or margarine, divided
3 Tbsp. cornstarch
1 cup beef bouillon
2 tsp. lemon juice
1/2 tsp. salt
1/4 tsp. Tabasco sauce
1/8 tsp. nutmeg

4 egg yolks
1/3 cup grated Parmesan cheese
2 Tbsp. chopped scallions
1 10-oz. package. frozen chopped
*   broccoli, or fresh broccoli, cooked*
5 egg whites
1/2 tsp. cream of tartar

Melt 3 tablespoons butter in pan; blend in cornstarch. Gradually stir in bouillon. Cook, stirring constantly, until mixture thickens and comes to a boil. Remove from heat. Stir in lemon juice, salt, Tabasco and nutmeg. Beat egg yolks in small bowl and stir in a little hot sauce. Stir into remaining sauce and add grated cheese. Melt remaining 1 tablespoon butter in skillet; add scallions and cook until tender. Add thawed broccoli; stir over moderately high heat until moisture evaporates, then add to sauce.

Beat egg whites with cream of tartar until stiff but not dry. Stir about one quarter of the beaten egg whites into the broccoli sauce; mix well. Fold in remaining whites, mixing as little as possible. Turn into buttered 1 1/2-quart soufflé dish and sprinkle top with more grated Parmesan cheese. Bake in 375°F oven 35–40 minutes, until top is puffed and browned. (Center will be moist; for a drier, firmer center, bake until a knife inserted in center comes out clean.) Serve with cheese sauce. Serves 6.

Cheese Sauce:

2 Tbsp. butter	1/4 tsp. Tabasco
1/2 tsp. salt	11/2 cups milk
1/8 tsp. dry mustard	1 cup Cheddar cheese, shredded
2 Tbsp. flour	

Melt butter in pan; blend in flour and seasonings. Stir in milk. Cook, stirring constantly, until mixture thickens and comes to a boil. Cook 2 minutes longer, stirring constantly. Add cheese; stir until melted.

Southern Corn Pudding

A real old-fashioned Southern dinner would include fried chicken with gravy, rice, corn pudding, sliced ripe tomato salad, hot biscuits with guava jelly, and for dessert, a richly frosted Lane Cake or homemade peach ice cream. Corn pudding and barbecued chicken were traditional partners at political gatherings in the early South.

2 cups milk	1 tsp. salt
2 cups corn, cut from the cob	1/4 tsp. pepper
1/4 cup melted butter	3 eggs, well beaten
1 Tbsp. sugar	

Combine milk and corn in saucepan and heat. Beat eggs; set aside. Add to milk and corn the butter, sugar and seasonings. Pour a little corn mixture over the beaten eggs. Beat this, then return to corn mixture. Stir and cook for several minutes. Turn into a greased casserole and bake in 350°F oven about 45 minutes, or until pudding sets. Serves 6.

Hot Bollos, Spanish Style

2 lbs. dried black-eyed peas	1 tsp. salt
1/4 tsp. pepper	seeds of small, dried hot pepper
3 cloves garlic	water
3 Tbsp. scraped onion	olive or cooking oil

Wash and pick peas; soak overnight in cold water. Rub peas against sides of a sieve until hulls come off. Wash again, scooping off hulls that float on top. Drain peas, mix with other ingredients except cooking oil. Chop in food processor using fine blade. Add enough water to make a thick paste; form into small balls. Fry balls in deep cooking oil at 375°F until golden brown. Serve as a hot appetizer. (Recipe borrowed from Cubans in Key West, where hot Bollos are sold on street corners.)

Lemon gives a tropical taste to Frosty Lemon Milk Sherbet

DESSERTS

Frosty Lemon Milk Sherbet

2 cups evaporated milk
1¹/₂ cups sugar
2 cups water
2 Tbsp. fresh mint, chopped
¹/₂ cup fresh lemon juice

³/₄ tsp. lemon rind, grated
2 tsp. vanilla
¹/₂ tsp. ground mace
¹/₈ tsp. salt
grated fresh lemon rind

Pour evaporated milk into freezing tray. Place in freezer and chill until frozen around sides, about 1 hour. Combine sugar, water and fresh mint in pan. Bring to boiling point; boil 2–3 minutes. Remove from heat; cool. Stir in lemon juice, lemon rind, vanilla, ground mace and salt. Turn into freezing tray and freeze to a mush, about 1 hour. Whip partially frozen evaporated milk until thick and fluffy. Gradually beat in frozen lemon mixture. Return to two freezing trays and freeze until firm. Garnish with grated lemon rind. Serves 8.

GUAVA SHELLS WITH CREAM CHEESE

One of the most delicious—and wonderfully simple—desserts in Florida is a gift from Spanish settlers. Pretty pink guava shells are sold in the gourmet section of most grocery stores. Simply open the can, serve them with or without the spicy juice, with a generous wedge of cream cheese. If you like, add a very salty crisp cracker for flavor contrast. A compliment-winner!

Papaya Nut Pie

1 cup orange juice
2 tablespoons cornstarch
1/4 cup sugar
juice of 1 lemon
1/2 tsp. ground ginger

1 1/2 cups diced papaya, fresh or canned
9-inch pie shell, baked
whipped cream
toasted coconut

Blend orange juice, cornstarch, sugar, lemon and ginger; heat slowly in pan, stirring constantly until thick and clear. Cool slightly. Pour over papaya cubes placed in baked pie shell. Refrigerate and chill well. Swirl whipped cream on top and sprinkle with toasted coconut before serving. Makes 1 pie.

Banana-Rum Pudding with Meringue

3 cups milk
1/3 cup cornstarch
1 cup sugar, divided
3/4 tsp. salt, divided
3 egg yolks, beaten

1 tsp. vanilla
1 tsp. rum flavoring
26 small vanilla wafers
3 large bananas
3 egg whites

Mix cornstarch with 2/3 cup sugar and 1/2 teaspoon salt. Scald milk in top of double boiler; pour slowly over cornstarch mixture. Cook over boiling water, stirring constantly, until mixture thickens. Cover; cook 15 minutes, stirring occasionally. Add hot mixture very slowly to beaten egg yolks, stirring constantly. Return mixture to double boiler; cook 2 minutes. Cool; add vanilla and rum flavoring. In 1 1/2-quart casserole, place alternate layers of wafers, bananas and pudding, ending with pudding. Add 1/4 teaspoon salt to egg whites; beat until foamy. Gradually add 1/3 cup sugar, beating until soft peaks form. Pile egg whites on pudding; bake in 350°F oven for 10–15 minutes or until light brown. Chill. Serves 6. ❧

2 *Florida Gold Coast*

Excitement was high in 1908 when the first automobile traveled from Jacksonville to Miami in five days.

We know that Indians lived near Biscayne Bay in 1513, because Ponce de Leon reported seeing them when he sailed into the Bay and discovered Cape Florida. Some of the bones and broken tools found there date back to 400–1400 A.D. At the mouth of the then clear-blue Miami River, a group of missionaries settled in 1568. Soldiers built Fort Dallas there in 1836.

But the Keys were where the action was. A handful of people attempted to start a coconut plantation among the mangroves, seagrape and scrub palmetto of Miami Beach in 1882. But insects plagued the workers; rats and rabbits ate the young tree shoots. By 1890 it was given up as a failure. Happily, enough trees survived to make Miami Beach a palm-fringed island.

In Miami, meanwhile, William Brickell built a home on the river's south shore while Julia Tuttle settled on the north side. She was the lady who put Miami on the map the day she cut an orange blossom, packed it in damp cotton, and sent it to Henry Flagler in north Florida. This ambitious lady had been urging him to extend his railroad to Miami, but he ignored her until the winter of 1894, when a hard freeze killed north Florida citrus.

The blossoms lured Flagler southward, where he verified that Miami was indeed basking in the sunshine far from icy breezes. He accepted gifts of land from Mrs. Tuttle and other residents, and his railroad was built. It was to bring guests to his new wooden Royal Palm Hotel in Miami, as it did to his Ponce de Leon in St. Augustine and his Royal Poinciana in Palm Beach.

While millionaires were enjoying bay breezes at Flagler's Royal Palm Hotel, Miami Beach was beginning to stir into life. Some dredging was done and the longest wooden bridge in the nation was begun by John S. Collins, then stopped when funds ran out. Millionaire promoter Carl F. Fisher of Indianapolis loaned him $50,000 with 200 acres of land as security, and the bridge was completed.

Fisher's promotional genius lured wealthy men south, persuaded them to invest, and began the development of land and building of hotels.

In the early 1920s, people by the millions came to Miami and Miami Beach, eager to make a fortune in the fantastic Florida land boom which peaked in 1925. To the Southerners who had made their home were added Latins and people from industrial centers in the north and midwest.

When, in 1926, the railroad broke down and a sunken ship blocked the harbor, preventing delivery of tons of building supplies, the boom went bust. The final misfortune was the great hurricane of September 18, 1926. It wiped out homes, killed hundreds, and pushed water from the ocean over to the bay.

Tourism—based on the new idea of package vacations for moderate-income families—revived the area and brought back a prosperity that has seldom faltered. Air conditioning extended the vacation season from winter throughout the summer. And the population continued to climb.

In 1973, when seven and a half years of Freedom Flights from Cuba ended, some 260,000 Cuban refugees had reached Miami. Desperate Cubans continued making the risky voyage in small boats and flimsy rafts—even inner-tube rafts—until by 1994, Dade County's population soared to nearly two million. Southwest Eighth Street became Little Havana and Spanish was the language of choice.

Miami continues to grow, with tourists from South America and Europe making Miami International Airport one of the busiest in the country. In downtown Miami, a people mover whisks visitors to theatres, restaurants and museums. In Miami Beach, picturesque hotels built in the '30s form the nucleus of an Art Deco district where sidewalk jazz concerts enliven the night. The Miami

Dolphins football team now has its own stadioum, seating 75,000, in north Dade County.

Once a sleepy Southern town, Miami is now home to long-time American residents as well as Columbians, Peruvians, Venezuelans, Panamanians, Puerto Ricans, and Cubans. It has become a major metropolis—the Gateway to Latin America.

One of the nation's largest Jewish communities began growing on the Beach; by 1947, nearly half the permanent population was Jewish. Refugees fleeing Castro's regime flowed into Miami by the hundreds of thousands. The imprint of both groups is reflected in the communities, and especially in the many fine Jewish and Spanish restaurants in south Florida.

Follow the beach from Miami Beach and you reach Fort Lauderdale, the boating capital of the world, with 135 miles of waterways. Here is Port Everglades, deepest harbor on Florida's east coast. The city was named to honor Major William Lauderdale, who commanded the local fort during the Seminole War.

The wide, white beach leads north to Palm Beach. Great mansions drowse in the beautiful seaside resort where Flagler built his hotel for millionaires in 1893. Addison Mizner's architectural touch remains, revealed in the mellow-toned red tile roofs and Spanish arches of the aging but still beautiful mansions. Worth Avenue is still one of the world's most beautiful streets.

Though it remains a favorite spot with many of America's socialites, inflation has struck and many of the great homes of Palm Beach have become museums or have been replaced by commercial buildings. But the food in elegant Palm Beach restaurants is still among the world's best.

Northward, the beach curves inward beside Fort Pierce, Melbourne and to John F. Kennedy Space Center. From the Center, the first moon landing by Apollo 11 was made in 1969, followed by six moon shots. In 1981, the first manned space shuttle launches were made. Next came the launch of the first five-member crew in 1983. In 1986, disaster struck when the space shuttle *Challenger* exploded after takeoff and all seven astronauts were killed, including a teacher who planned to teach from space.

It was not until two years later that the space program resumed. Today, rocket-powered probes venture deep into space, exploring distant planets and expanding scientists' knowledge of the universe. Weather satellites stationed in space have revolutionized weather reporting and communications, and scientific experiments in space enable teams to spend long periods in spacecrafts with scientists from other countries, including Russia.

South Florida's food is a world unto itself. The nation's only true subtropical area produces exotic mangoes, avocados, limes, lychee nuts, coconuts, as well as a full array of winter vegetables. Seafood is plentiful, with stone crabs, lobster, red snapper, and mackerel among the favorites.

Great chefs practice their art in luxury hotels and gourmet restaurants on Florida's east coast, delighting local residents as well as tourists from all over the world.

SPANISH SPECIALTIES

Frijoles Negros a la Cubana (Cuban Black Beans)

2 cups (1 lb.) black beans	1 bay leaf
water, sufficient to cover beans	1 green pepper, minced
1/2 tsp. salt, or to taste	1 onion, chopped
1 clove garlic, cut in half	1 Tbsp. cider vinegar
2 Tbsp. olive oil	salt, pepper to taste
3 cloves garlic, mashed	fluffy white rice

Wash and pick beans. Place in covered pot with enough water to stand one inch above beans. Soak overnight. Add salt and garlic halves and cook beans until tender. Meanwhile, to make sauce, heat oil in heavy frying pan and add mashed garlic, bay leaf, green pepper and onion. Lower heat to simmer and cook 5 minutes. Add vinegar and salt to taste. Mix with beans and reheat until hot. Serve with fluffy white rice. Serves 6.

Eggs in Spanish Sauce

Combining rice with eggs in this fashion is popular in old Spain as well as in Latin American countries.

1 29-oz. can tomatoes	1/2 bay leaf
1 sliced onion	2 Tbsp. butter or margarine
1 tsp. sugar	2 Tbsp. flour
3/4 tsp. Tabasco	3 cups cooked rice
3/4 tsp. salt	6 eggs
1/8 tsp. ground cloves	1/4 cup grated Cheddar cheese

Simmer tomatoes, onion, sugar, Tabasco, salt, cloves and bay leaf in saucepan about 10 minutes. Remove bay leaf. Blend butter and flour together. Add to tomato mixture. Cook, stirring constantly, until thickened. Spread rice in greased shallow 2½-quart casserole, making 6 hollows in it with a tablespoon. Break an egg into each nest. Carefully pour sauce over all. Sprinkle with cheese. Bake in 350°F oven 20 minutes or until the eggs are firm. Serves 6.

Green Banana Puree

Sometimes called plantains, green or cooking bananas are a Cuban staple. They are also delicious sliced, sprinkled with sugar and sauteed in a little butter.

6 large, green, firm cooking bananas
lemon juice

4 cups water
½ tsp. salt

Peel green bananas; scrape them to remove the fibrous strings, then rub them with lemon juice. Boil in salted water until tender. Drain and mash. Serve in a mound on a hot dish to accompany meats. Serves 6.

Cuban Flan (Caramel Custard)

¾ cup sugar, divided
1 tsp. water
pinch of salt

2 cups milk
4 egg yolks
½ tsp. vanilla

In skillet, over very low heat, place 6 tablespoons sugar and the water and cook until sugar turns to golden syrup. Stir occasionally to prevent burning. Pour into four custard cups and cool until firm. Beat together milk, beaten egg yolks, vanilla and 2 tablespoons sugar until thoroughly blended. Pour over caramel in custard cups. Pour ½ inch boiling water in deep pan; place cups in water. Bake at 325°F about 1 hour 15 minutes, or until knife slipped into center comes out clean. Chill well. Invert onto chilled plates to serve. Serves 4.

GOLD COAST GOURMET

Curried Egg Mold

2 envelopes unflavored gelatin
1¹/2 cup cold water
2 cups rich chicken stock, boiling
1 Tbsp. curry powder

1¹/2 cups mayonnaise
3 sliced hard-cooked eggs
6 sliced stuffed olives
¹/2 cup finely sliced celery

Sprinkle gelatin on cold water until soft. Add gelatin mixture and curry powder to chicken stock. Stir to dissolve. Chill till slightly thick. Gradually stir in mayonnaise until blended. Mix in eggs, olives, celery. Season to taste with salt and pepper. Turn into oiled 1¹/2-quart ring mold. Chill until firm; unmold on greens. If desired, garnish with green mayonnaise and black olives. Serves 6–8.

Chicken Avocado Crepes

¹/2 cup ripe olives, chopped
5 Tbsp. butter
5 Tbsp. flour
1 cup cream (or undiluted
  evaporated milk)
1 cup chicken broth
³/4 cup dry white wine
1 cup grated Swiss cheese
¹/2 tsp. Worcestershire sauce
2 Tbsp. chopped parsley

salt, pepper
2 cups diced cooked chicken
2 eggs
²/3 cup milk
¹/2 cup sifted flour
¹/2 tsp. salt
1 Tbsp. melted butter
1 large avocado, peeled and sliced
paprika, ripe olives for garnish

In large saucepan, melt 5 tablespoons butter and blend in 5 tablespoons flour. Pour in cream, broth and wine. Cook, stirring constantly, until it boils and thickens. Stir in ³/4 cup cheese, Worcestershire sauce, parsley, and salt and pepper to taste; stir until smooth. Reserve 1 cup sauce; add olives and chicken to the rest.

To make crepes, beat eggs lightly; combine with milk. Sift ¹/2 cup flour with ¹/2 teaspoon salt. Combine with egg mixture; beat until smooth. Beat in melted butter. In lightly greased frying pan, pour 4 tablespoons batter; tilt pan to spread. Cook until golden brown, turning once. Repeat.

In greased baking dish, place crepes which have been filled with sauce, rolled and secured with toothpick. Pour reserved sauce over crepes; sprinkle with remaining cheese and paprika. Bake in 375°F oven 15 minutes; then place under the broiler for a couple of minutes to brown. Top crepes with sliced avocado and whole ripe olives. Serves 6.

JFK Salad Dressing

(Created by Fontainebleau Hotel chef at Miami Beach for John F. Kennedy.)

5 whole eggs
1 clove garlic
1 tsp. salt
1/4 tsp. pepper
2 Tbsp. paprika

1 tsp. prepared mustard
3 cups salad oil
1 cup olive oil
1/2 cup red wine vinegar

Crack eggs into bowl. Crush garlic and add. Combine with salt, pepper, paprika and mustard; mix well. Add oils slowly, beating constantly. If mixture gets too thick, add a little vinegar. Continue beating, adding all of the vinegar until thoroughly blended. Correct salt, pepper to taste. Makes 6 cups.

Italian Meat Loaf

3 slices white bread
3 slices rye bread
1 1/4 cups beef stock
4 Tbsp. minced onion
1 Tbsp. prepared mustard
2 tsp. salt

1/2 tsp. parsley flakes
1/8 tsp. black pepper
1/4 cup Parmesan cheese
2 eggs
2 lbs. ground beef
1 Tbsp. butter

Break bread into pieces in large mixing bowl. Add beef stock and onion. Let stand 10 minutes. With fork, mash bread pieces and beat mixture well. Add mustard, salt, parsley flakes, pepper, cheese, eggs. Beat well with a fork. Add beef; mix thoroughly. Pack into oiled, 9- x 5-inch loaf pan. Dot top with butter. Bake in 375°F oven 60–70 minutes. Serves 8.

Ham-Cheese Fondue Soufflé

3 cups French or Italian bread, cubed
3 cups cooked ham, cubed
1/2 lb. Cheddar cheese, in 1-inch cubes
3 tablespoons flour
1 Tbsp. dry mustard

3 Tbsp. butter, melted
4 eggs
3 cups milk
few drops red hot sauce

Butter an 8-cup, straight-sided casserole dish. In bottom, place a layer of cubed bread, then a layer of ham, then a layer of cubed cheese. Mix flour with mustard; sprinkle over cheese. Drizzle butter or margarine over top. Beat eggs; add milk and red hot sauce; pour over layers in casserole dish. Cover; chill at least 4 hours, preferably overnight. Bake uncovered in 350°F oven I hour. Serve at once. (The secret of this dish is the long chilling.) Serves 6.

JEWISH SPECIALTIES

Sauerbraten with Potato Pancakes

4 lb. round steak
1 pint cider vinegar
water
3 bay leaves
3 peppercorns
2 Tbsp. flour
salt, pepper, paprika

1 tsp. allspice
2 Tbsp. cooking oil
6 carrots
6 onions, sliced
12 gingersnaps
1 Tbsp. sugar

Place meat in bowl, pour over vinegar and enough water to cover. Add bay leaves and peppercorns. Refrigerate 3 days. Combine flour, salt, pepper, paprika and allspice. Drain meat; shake in bag filled with flour mixture. Brown meat lightly in hot oil. Place meat in heavy saucepan with sliced carrots, onions and 2 cups of vinegar marinade. Cover and simmer 2 hours. Crumble gingersnaps; add gingersnaps and sugar to liquid around meat. Add salt and pepper to taste. Serve with potato pancakes. Serves 6.

Potato Pancakes (Latkes)

2 cups potatoes
2 eggs, well beaten
1 Tbsp. flour or matzo meal
vegetable oil

pinch baking powder
1 Tbsp. grated onion
salt, pepper to taste

Peel and grate potatoes. Thoroughly combine all ingredients. Drop by tablespoonfuls into hot oil in frying pan. Fry until crisp at edges on under side; turn and fry until done. Serves 4.

Quick Blini (Russian Pancakes)

3/4 cup sifted all-purpose flour
1/3 tsp. baking powder
1/4 tsp. salt

1/2 cup milk
1 slightly beaten egg
1 pint (2 cups) sour cream

Sift together twice the flour, baking powder, and salt. Stir in remaining ingredients; mix well. Drop by tablespoon to make very small, very thin pancakes, 2 inches wide or less. Brown on hot griddle, turning once. Serve garnished with dollops of sour cream. Makes 25–30 pancakes.

Passover Jelly Roll

½ cup sifted matzo cake meal
½ cup potato flour
6 eggs, separated
1 cup sugar
juice and rind of ½ lemon

2 Tbsp. cold water
¼ tsp. salt
1 cup raspberry preserves
confectioners' sugar

Line a 10- x 15-inch jelly roll pan with wax paper. Sift together matzo cake meal and potato flour. Beat egg yolks with sugar until thick and lemon-colored. Stir in lemon juice, grated rind and water. Gradually add sifted dry ingredients, stirring to make a thick batter. Beat egg whites and salt until stiff but not dry. Fold gently into batter.

Turn batter into jelly roll pan. Bake in 325°F oven about 20 minutes or until just done. Don't let edges brown and harden. Remove from oven; peel off paper. Turn onto a towel which has been spread with sugar. Trim off crisp edges. Roll cake in towel; cool completely. Unroll. Remove towel. Spread with preserves. Roll again; dust lightly with confectioners' sugar. Serves 10.

TROPICAL FRUIT SPECIALTIES

Caracas Pineapple Coupe

2 fresh pineapples
1 cantaloupe
1/4 cup maraschino cordial
1/4 cup Cointreau cordial

1 pint orange sherbet
1 pint lime sherbet
1/4 cup shredded coconut
1/2 pint heavy cream, whipped

Cut pineapples in half lengthwise; scoop out center, leaving 1/2-inch border of fruit around edge. Dice scooped-out pineapple. Cut cantaloupe, clean, and cut meat into balls or cubes. Combine the two cordials, pineapple chunks and cantaloupe balls; refrigerate for 4 hours. Fill pineapple shells with fruit. Top with orange and lime sherbets, sprinkle with shredded coconut and circle with whipped cream. Serves 4 generously.

Mango Frost

Deceptively simple, this recipe is an all-time favorite. Especially good after a heavy meal, it has marvelous tropical flavor and a texture like soft sherbet. Peaches may be substituted for the mangoes, if you like.

1 heaping cup sliced mangoes
2 Tbsp. powdered milk
juice of 1 lime

1 Tbsp. sugar
1 Tbsp. light rum
crushed ice

Combine first 5 ingredients in blender. Add crushed ice to fill container. Blend at high speed until mixture thickens to the consistency of soft sherbet. Serve immediately topped with a sprig of mint, with a spoon or straw, depending on thickness. Serves 2.

Lime French Dressing

5 Tbsp. salad oil
1/2 tsp. salt
1/2 tsp. paprika
1/2 tsp. prepared mustard

6 Tbsp. lime juice
1 tsp. onion juice
1/2 tsp. garlic salt

Place all ingredients in small bottle; cover tightly and shake well. Chill. Process in blender just before serving. Makes 3/4 cup of tart dressing—perfect with greens, avocados or vegetable combinations.

Lime Dessert Sauce

1 Tbsp. cornstarch
1/2 cup sugar
cold water

3/4 cup boiling water
2 Tbsp. butter or margarine
2 1/2 Tbsp. lime juice

Mix cornstarch with sugar. Blend to smooth paste with a little cold water. Gradually stir paste into boiling water. Continue stirring over moderate heat until thickened. Remove from stove. Add butter and lime juice. This tangy, sweet sauce is delicious hot or cold, over pudding or fritters. Makes about 1 1/2 cups.

Florida Green Ice Cream

1 medium avocado, de-seeded and
   mashed (3/4 cup of pulp)
2/3 cup sugar
1/2 tsp. salt

3 1/2 Tbsp. lime juice
1 cup pineapple juice
1 1/2 cups light cream

Combine all ingredients and stir until thoroughly blended. Freeze in ice cube tray until almost firm. Break up and whip until light and fluffy. Turn into fancy one-quart mold and refreeze 2 hours or until firm. Serves 6.

Cream of Avocado Soup

1 quart thin white sauce
1 cup avocado pulp, finely mashed
1/6 tsp. ginger
pinch of salt

grated rind of 1 orange
6 Tbsp. heavy cream, whipped
paprika
12 thin slices of avocado

Combine white sauce, avocado, ginger, salt and orange rind. Beat until well blended. Heat but do not boil. Ladle soup into 6 individual serving bowls. Garnish with dollop of whipped cream, dash of paprika and thin slices of avocado. Serves 6.

Prize-Winning Shrimp-Stuffed Avocados

3 large avocados
3 Tbsp. lime juice
1 tsp. salt, divided
4 Tbsp. butter
6 Tbsp. flour
1/8 tsp. black pepper

1 1/2 cups milk
1/2 cup sliced, cooked celery
1/4 cup pimiento, minced
1 cup boiled shrimp
2/3 cup grated Cheddar cheese

Cut avocados in half lengthwise; peel and remove pit. Sprinkle with lime juice and 1/2 teaspoon salt. Melt butter, blend in flour, add remaining salt, pepper and milk; cook until thickened, stirring constantly. Add celery, pimiento and shrimp. Fill avocados with shrimp mixture; cover with grated cheese, place in baking pan. Pour boiling water in pan to a depth of 1/2 inch and bake in 350°F oven 15 minutes. Serves 6.

Kumquat (or Calamondin) Marmalade

1 quart kumquats, halved and seeded
1 cup sugar per cup of fruit
juice of 1/2 lemon

Place halved, seeded fruit in enough water to cover it; cook until skin is soft. Leave fruit in pan, cover and let soak in juices overnight. Measure 1 cup sugar to each cup of fruit. Add juice of half a lemon (or whole lemon for added tartness). Cook over very high heat until it boils, then start stirring and cook, stirring constantly, 15 minutes—but never more than 20 minutes! This makes a marmalade of soft consistency. Pour into jars and seal.

Surinam Cherry Jam

3 3/4 cups sugar
2 cups water
3 3/4 cups Surinam cherries, seeded

Combine sugar and water, bring to boil and add cherries. Boil cherries in syrup 20–25 minutes, or until juice thickens slightly but does not jell. Pour into hot jars and seal.

Bananas Flambé

3 Tbsp. butter
2 Tbsp. brown sugar
3 bananas, peeled, sliced lengthwise

1/4 cup banana liqueur
1/4 cup light rum
2 Tbsp. brandy

Melt butter in chafing dish or frying pan. Add brown sugar and cook until bubbling and syrupy. Put in sliced bananas, roll in sauce and spoon sauce over until glazed. Push bananas to one side; heat other side of pan until it is dry. Pour in banana liqueur; ignite. Spoon flaming liqueur over fruit until flames die. Repeat with rum, then brandy, each time letting flames die. Serve over vanilla ice cream. Serves 3.

Guava Cheese Pie

1/2 cup guava paste
1/2 cup cream
3 eggs
1 lb. sieved cottage cheese

1 Tbsp. lime juice
pinch of salt
8-inch graham cracker crumb crust
dash of mace

Chop guava paste into small cubes. Heat in cream over lowest possible heat until paste partially melts but tiny blobs of paste remain. Beat eggs well until fluffy and lemon colored. Add to cheese together with guava mixture, lime juice, salt. Pour into crumb crust; sprinkle with mace. Bake in 350°F. oven 45–55 minutes. Makes one 8-inch pie.

Papaya Sundae

¼ cup honey
¼ cup cream
½ cup sugar
1 Tbsp. butter or margarine
¼ cup lime or lemon juice

½ cup sweetened, flaked coconut
1 papaya
1 quart vanilla ice cream
garnishes: mint sprigs, stemmed
    cherries

Combine honey, cream, sugar and butter. Boil 3 minutes, stirring constantly. Chill. Stir in lime juice and coconut. Halve papaya; scoop out seeds and membrane. Peel; cut crosswise into ½-inch slices. Scoop ice cream into sundae dishes and encircle it with papaya slices. Pour sauce on top, or serve it at the table. Garnish with mint and cherries. Serves 6.

Mango Chutney, Indian Style

4 lbs. green mangoes
2 quarts vinegar
2 lbs. sugar
2 Tbsp. white mustard seed
1 Tbsp. ground dried chili pepper

4 tsp. allspice
2 cups dark raisins
1 clove garlic
1 lb. preserved ginger in syrup

Peel and cut fruit; add I quart vinegar. Boil 20 minutes. Combine sugar and second quart of vinegar and boil until thick syrup forms, about I hour. Pour off most of the liquid from fruit and add to this syrup. Boil this combination until thickened, about 15 minutes. Combine this thick syrup with the rest of the ingredients and fruit except ginger; cook 30 minutes. Add chopped ginger and its syrup; cook 10 minutes longer. Remove garlic. Pour into sterilized jars and seal. To improve flavor, let stand in the sun for three days. Makes about 4 quarts.

FREEZING MANGOES

Use high quality mangoes at peak of ripeness. Peel and cut from seed in slices. Pack into moisture-vapor-proof containers, packing down to eliminate air spaces. Leave ¾-inch space at top. Pour sweetened limeade over to cover. (This prevents fruit from drying out and losing texture and flavor.) Seal and freeze, placing against walls of home freezer.

The tropical taste of pineapple flavors a tangy cheese dip.

Pineapple Cheese Dip

8 oz. whipped cream cheese
2 cups shredded Cheddar cheese
1/4 cup milk
3 Tbsp. white Port wine (or grape juice)

1 tsp. Worcestershire sauce
1/2 tsp. salt
1 ripe sweet pineapple
1/2 tsp. dry mustard

Beat together cheeses, milk, wine, Worcestershire sauce, salt, and dry mustard in bowl. Cut pineapple in half crosswise and cut pineapple meat out of bottom half to make a shell; cut meat into cubes. Fill shell with cheese mixture. Refrigerate until ready to serve. Cut crown off top half of pineapple, cut off rind, cut into quarters, cut away core and cut meat into chunks. Refrigerate. Let cheese-stuffed pineapple stand at room temperature for 15 minutes to soften before serving. Place on serving plate and surround with pineapple chunks. Spear pineapple chunks with cocktail picks and dip into cheese mixture. Makes about 2 1/2 cups cheese dip.

Val Mayfield's Tropical Fruit Pie

Crust:
2 cups almond macaroon crumbs
¼ cup confectioners' sugar
½ cup melted butter or margarine

Filling:

1 cup crushed pineapple
2 Tbsp. flour
5 Tbsp. sugar, divided
1½ cups fresh or frozen coconut
½ tsp. coconut flavoring

2 large bananas, peeled and brushed
   with lemon juice
1 cup heavy cream, whipped
maraschino cherries

In medium bowl, toss macaroon crumbs, confectioners' sugar and butter with fork until well mixed. Press mixture into bottom and sides of 8-inch pie plate. Refrigerate.

Combine pineapple, flour and 3 tablespoons sugar in saucepan and cook over medium heat until thickened, stirring constantly, about 10 minutes. Cool.

Open coconut, remove the meat and grate it. Mix grated coconut with 2 tablespoons sugar and flavoring. Toast ½ cup of sweetened, flavored coconut lightly in 250°F oven; set the rest aside.

Slice the bananas and arrange them in the bottom of the pie crust. Spread cooled pineapple mixture over bananas. Cover with one cup untoasted coconut. Top with whipped cream. Sprinkle with ½ cup toasted coconut. Refrigerate. Just before serving, garnish with maraschino cherries. Makes one 8-inch pie. ✤

HOW TO OPEN A COCONUT

To open fresh coconut, first make a hole in the eye and drain out the milk. Place nut in 350°F oven 20 minutes. Remove; let cool. Wrap coconut in a towel and crack it with a hammer—one easy pull and the meat is out. Peel the brown skin away from the meat. Refrigerate unused coconut and milk.

3 *Colorful Florida Keys*

Pigeon Key lies in the shadow of the Overseas Highway,
which travels more than 100 miles out in the Gulf to reach Key West.

No romantic novel could have a plot more exciting than the real-life history of the Florida Keys, a chain of white coral islands strung in a half moon from the mainland to Key West. Like a hair-raising adventure tale, it bristles with violence and sudden death, alternating with times of peace and prosperity.

Early Spanish adventurers exploring all the way to the southernmost island found piles of human bones, presumably men slain during a battle with the fierce, near-naked Calusas. They named the place Cayo Hueso—Bone Key—which was corrupted to "Key West."

In 1513, Ponce de Leon sailed past the rocky islands and gave them a highly appropriate name, Los Martires, because they looked like suffering men.

Ponce de Leon claimed Florida for Spain when he came searching for gold and the Fountain of Youth. After he failed and died, followed by de Soto, the King of Spain abandoned the idea of settling Florida and moved his ships to Mexico and South America to loot them of gold, silver, jewels and precious woods.

Twice a year, these treasure-laden ships passed through the Bahama Channel and the treacherous, reef-bound water along the Keys, and brought the Keys their most despicable residents—cut-throat English pirates and French buccaneers who preyed on stricken ships and attacked unwary ones, torturing and killing crews and leaving few survivors. Thousands of ships went down.

Later, when the English won Florida, piracy continued, but with English ships plundered by Spanish pirates. From 1812 to 1823, records show there were 3,007 piracies, about one a day!

Perhaps the most infamous of all the pirates was a huge, fearsome former slave called Black Caesar. A myth he may be, but not to many Keys oldtimers who contend that he lived and plied his grisly career out of Caesar's Creek between Old Rhodes and Elliott Keys north of Key Largo.

The Calusa Indians joined in the pirating. They were finally destroyed by Creek Indians instructed by the settlers from Georgia to bring back slaves who had taken refuge with the Florida Indians, and to kill Calusas. By 1765, the Calusas were gone.

Piracy did not end until 1823, when Commodore David Porter drove the buccaneers from the Keys with a "mosquito fleet." In 1821, Spain ceded East and West Florida to the U.S. and Andrew Jackson became territorial governor. Florida became a state in 1845.

The 1830s were a hectic boom period in Key West. Ships were still being wrecked in the treacherous waters. Licenses were issued giving a ship's cargo to the first salvage crew reaching it, and all around the city, great piles of furniture, clothing, jewels and cargo went to the highest bidder.

In 1890, Key West was the richest city per capita in the U.S., and had the largest population in Florida—18,000. When Federal lighthouses stopped the wrecks, the boom was over.

Before the Civil War, when Florida seceded from the Union, Key West remained in Union hands and fort-building began in this Gibraltar of the Caribbean. The beautiful old handmade brick of Fort Taylor on the island and Fort Jefferson, 60 miles west on Dry Tortugas, are now tourists' delights.

At one time, Key West was the nation's top producer of fine Havana cigars, before a great fire caused the plant to be moved to Tampa's Ybor City.

A new era began for the Keys when Henry Flagler's dream railroad spanned 128 miles of land and sea from Homestead to Key West, and the first train arrived carrying Flagler in 1912. One thousand school children sang a welcome; Flagler cried.

World-famous sportsmen flocked to the Keys; new towns sprang up; new residents poured in. By 1913, Key West had 22,000 residents. Then the Labor Day hurricane of 1935 wiped out the railroad, killed hundreds, and washed out much of the one road that linked the keys to the mainland.

Even with the building of a new Overseas Highway, prosperity did not return until World War II. By 1990, Key West had 24,800.

Life on the Keys bred a special kind of men and women—hardy people with valor and toughness of pioneers. A strong Cockney accent identifies many of them with the Englishmen who first left the Bahamas for the Keys to cut scarce wood and find turtles. Proudly they call themselves "Conchs" after the rose-pink shellfish that once was a staple in the Keys diet.

They built humble but sturdy dwellings on the white coral islands that seem to float on the blue-green sea. And they survived on food from the sea, canned foods brought in by boat, coconuts, precious garden vegetables and fruit from the hardy little Key lime trees. Life was lonely and secluded, but they loved it.

Because there was no refrigeration, canned condensed milk was in great demand. With it, the Conchs produced a true masterpiece, Key Lime Pie.

Their fish was plentiful: crawfish (Florida spiny lobster), stone crabs, grunt, snapper, grouper, sea trout, bonefish, mackerel, kingfish, and pink jumbo shrimp. Great green sea turtles weighing up to 300 pounds were a major food source. Today, all sea turtles are protected species, and so is the Queen Conch that gave the Keys pioneers their nickname.

Conch foods are a fascinating blend of Southern Cracker cooking, zesty Latin, and spicy Caribbean. Conch seafood is a world away from simple New England dishes—but it is spectacularly good.

Woven into the cuisine are tropical foods such as avocado, plantain, carissa, kumquat, guava, papaya, pineapple, coconut. Many of these meld with seafood into unforgettable salads. But the most memorable dish of all is, of course, Key Lime Pie. Just be sure when you try it on the Keys, to ask for the original recipe made with sweetened condensed milk. Conchs consider this the *only* one, and all variations as outrageous imitations.

No trip to Key West would be complete without observing an old tradition: visiting Mallory Square at sunset when street vendors sell banana bread—as musicians, bicycle riders and artists gather on the dock to salute the sun as it sinks into the ocean in crimson and golden splendor.

The tropical beauty and unexcelled fishing of Key West have lured many celebrities including the late President Truman, literary greats Ernest Hemingway and Tennessee Williams. Visitors jam the old city to see the picturesque cedar and hardwood homes built by seafaring men, to attend Wreckers' Balls and other events during fun-filled old Island Days in mid-winter. The city has retained its quaint charm—a tropical oasis unlike any other.

KEYS SEAFOOD RECIPES

Crawfish Chelow (Florida Lobster)

Eat this in soup bowls with Tender-Crust Cuban Bread (page 49).

2 medium onions, chopped
6 cloves garlic, finely chopped
1 large green pepper, chopped
1/4–1/3 cup olive oil
2 8-oz. cans tomato sauce
1 6-oz. can tomato paste

1 tsp. salt
1/8 tsp. pepper
3 bay leaves
1/4 tsp. oregano
4 large or 6 small crawfish

Fry onions, garlic, green pepper in oil until tender but not browned, stirring occasionally. Use enough oil to prevent scorching. Add tomato sauce and tomato paste. Rinse each can with a tablespoon or two of water, and add this water to the stew. Add salt, pepper, bay leaves, oregano. Remove crawfish from shells, chop in small pieces and add. Cook, uncovered, about 20 minutes, until slightly cooked down. Serve hot in soup bowls. Serves 6.

Minced Crawfish

Minced crawfish is similar to chelow but less soupy. It is served over white rice and accompanied by black beans, green salad and Cuban bread.

1/2 large green pepper, chopped
1/2 large onion, chopped
6 small cloves garlic, finely chopped
3 Tbsp. oil, bacon drippings, or
    shortening
2 bay leaves

4 large or 6 small crawfish
1 8-oz. can tomato sauce
1/4 tsp. oregano
1 1/2 tsp. Worcestershire sauce
1 tsp. salt
1/8 tsp. pepper

Fry green pepper, onion and garlic in oil until tender but not browned, stirring now and then. Use more oil, if needed, to prevent scorching. Remove crawfish from shells and cut fine. Add to onion mixture with bay leaves and stir. Cook until very hot, about 3 minutes. Add tomato sauce and a little water to rinse can. Add oregano, Worcestershire sauce, salt and pepper. Cook uncovered about 15 minutes, until some of the liquid has cooked out. Minced crawfish should be moist, but not runny with juice. Serve over hot, fluffy rice. Serves 8.

Conch Chowder

Queen Conchs may not be taken from Florida waters, but may be purchased at some seafood markets. They are imported from the Caribbean where they are raised commercially.

1/4 lb. salt pork	8 large conchs
2 medium onions, chopped	1 Tbsp. vinegar
4 cloves garlic, crushed	2 tsp. salt
1 large green pepper, chopped	1/2 tsp. pepper
1 16-oz. can tomatoes	1 Tbsp. oregano
1 6-oz. can tomato paste	4 bay leaves
2 quarts hot water	2 Tbsp. barbecue sauce
1 tsp. poultry seasoning	9 medium potatoes, peeled and sliced

Dice salt pork and fry in large pot. Add onions, garlic, green pepper. Cook until tender but not browned. Add tomatoes, tomato paste, hot water, poultry seasoning, cook over low heat while preparing conch.

Pound conchs with back of knife to break up tough tissue. Chop. Add to chowder. Bring to a boil. Add vinegar, salt, pepper, oregano, bay leaves and barbecue sauce. Cover and bring to a boil, then turn heat low and simmer 2 hours. Add potatoes and simmer until potatoes are tender, about 20 minutes. Serves 8 generously.

Dolphin Amandine

The fish that is usually called "dolphin" here is often sold under its Hawaiian name of "mahi-mahi." It is <u>not</u> the big, playful mammal that performs at Sea World.

12 1/2-inch thick dolphin fillets (about 6 oz. each)	1/8 tsp. white pepper
	1–1 1/2 tsp. paprika
1 Tbsp. cooking oil	1/2 cup (1 stick) butter
1 tsp. salt	1 6-oz. package slivered almonds

Place dolphin fillets in a lightly oiled shallow pan. No rack is needed. Sprinkle with salt, pepper and paprika. Cook 1 minute in center of electric oven, then 6–7 minutes close under broiler. If using a gas oven, cook 1 minute in upper part of oven, 6–7 minutes under broiler flame.

Meanwhile, melt butter. Add almonds and cook over very low heat about 5 minutes, until pale brown. Pour over hot dolphin and serve at once. Serves 12.

Baked Mackerel in Spanish Sauce

Key West families of Spanish origin use garlic freely, which must be done for authentic flavor. You may, of course, reduce it to suit your taste.

1 3-lb. King or Spanish Mackerel	1 Tbsp. onion, finely chopped
cooking oil	1 cup Spanish Sauce
salt and pepper	1/4 cup bread crumbs
1/2 cup tomato juice	2 Tbsp. butter

Clean fish, rub with cooking oil and season with salt and pepper. Place fish in oiled pan; pour on tomato juice, then sprinkle with onion. Bake at 350°F about 30 minutes, basting occasionally. Remove from oven; pour Spanish Sauce over fish, sprinkle top with bread crumbs and dot with butter. Place in oven until browned. Serves 6.

Spanish Sauce:

2 green peppers, coarsely chopped	2 bay leaves
5 cloves garlic, finely chopped	1/4 tsp. oregano
1/2 cup fresh, light olive oil	1 1/2 tsp. Worcestershire sauce
3 onions, coarsely chopped	juice of 1 lime
1 28-oz. can tomatoes	salt and pepper
1 10 1/2-oz. can tomato puree	

In saucepan, heat olive oil and cook garlic and green peppers until latter are almost tender. Add onion; cook until tender but not browned. Stir in tomatoes, tomato puree, bay leaves, oregano, Worcestershire sauce, lime juice and salt and pepper to taste. Simmer until well blended, about 20 minutes, stirring occasionally. Makes about 2 1/2 cups sauce.

Fried Florida Shrimp

For superb taste, use fresh Florida shrimp. If frozen shrimp are used, thaw before using. Shell, devein and bread shrimp, then refrigerate until chilled. (Tip: Cooking oil won't get too salty and can be reused if shrimp are salted after cooking.)

1 lb. Florida shrimp, cleaned	1/2 cup fine dry bread crumbs
1/4 cup flour	salt and pepper to taste
1/4 cup undiluted evaporated milk	cooking oil to fill pot 1/3 full

Shell and devein shrimp. Shake in flour placed in a small paper bag. Dip into milk, drain slightly, then coat with bread crumbs. Pat on until breading sticks firmly. Refrigerate. Fry in 375°F deep cooking oil until golden brown, about 3 minutes. Season with salt and pepper; serve at once. Serves 3 generously.

Ocean Reef Grouper Chowder

1 fresh grouper, about 5 lbs.	1 medium onion, finely chopped
1 gallon water	1 tsp. curry powder
1 Tbsp. salt	1/2 tsp. rosemary
1 large onion, coarsely chopped	1/2 tsp. oregano
4 whole cloves	1/2 tsp. leaf thyme
1 bay leaf	1 1/2 cups flour
1 large stalk celery, chopped	2 tsp. monosodium glutamate
1 stick butter	about 1 quart light cream

Clean grouper and cut off head. Place grouper with head in large kettle with water, salt, large onion, cloves, bay leaf and celery. Bring to a boil, reduce heat to simmer and cook about 12 minutes, or until fish flakes when pierced with a fork. Take pot off the heat; strain liquid. Remove fish from bones and cut in bite-size pieces. Saute onion in butter in a saucepan until tender but not brown. Add curry powder, rosemary, oregano, thyme, and flour, stirring until smooth. Stir in stock drained from grouper, and monosodium glutamate. Stir until smooth, then reduce to simmer and cook 20–25 minutes.

Using 1/3 as much cream as fish liquid, bring cream to boil in a separate pan. Pour cream into chowder; add grouper chunks. Reheat; serve at once. Makes 20 servings—enough for a chowder party. (Tip: freeze leftover chowder and reheat, but do not boil.)

Pompano Stew

1/2 lb. salt pork	4 medium potatoes
4 medium onions, chopped	1 1/2 quarts water
3 tomatoes, peeled and chopped	3 lb. pompano, cut in steaks
1 clove garlic	1 tsp. salt
1 small green pepper, chopped	1/8 tsp. pepper
1 cup celery, chopped	2 Tbsp. flour

Dice salt pork and fry. Add onions, tomatoes, garlic, green pepper and celery. Cook until tender, stirring occasionally. Add potatoes and water. Cover; cook until potatoes are tender, about 20 minutes. Add pompano, salt and pepper, and cook until tender, 10–15 minutes. Stir flour into a little water to make a smooth paste; stir into broth, cooking and stirring until thick and smooth. Serves 5–6.

Key West Paella

1/2 cup olive oil
4 cloves garlic
2 bay leaves
1 tsp. oregano
2 lb. chicken pieces
1/2 lb. diced pork loin
1 cup chopped onion
1 chorizo (hot Spanish sausage)
1/2 cup diced cooked ham
4 raw oysters
4 raw clams
8 raw shrimp, peeled and deveined

1 cup long grain rice
4 cups hot stock or water
1 1/2 tsp. salt
1/4 tsp. pepper
1 tsp. monosodium glutamate
1/4 tsp. powdered saffron
1 large green pepper, sliced
2–3 pimientos, halved
1 8-oz. can peas, drained
optional garnishes: hard-cooked eggs,
    asparagus

Heat olive oil in paella (large ovenproof casserole); saute garlic and bay leaves gently 3 minutes; remove. Add oregano, chicken and pork to oil and cook, turning until browned and almost done. Add onion, sausage (cut in inch-long pieces) and ham. Saute 3 minutes. Add oysters, clams, shrimp, rice, stock, salt, pepper, monosodium glutamate and saffron. (To use thread saffron, crush and heat in a spoonful of water held over the pot for a minute or two, then add.) Boil for 10 minutes. Arrange green pepper, pimientos, and peas on top for decoration. Cover and bake in 375°F oven for 15 minutes. Serves 6–8.

Shrimp Cocktail

Tip: Beware of overcooking. It makes shrimp tough.

1 lb. large shrimp
1 quart water
1 Tbsp. salt

1 Tbsp. vinegar
lettuce leaves
cocktail sauce

Wash shrimp in shells under cold running water. Drop into COLD water, allowing 1 tablespoon salt for each quart of water. When water boils, add a tablespoon of vinegar. Time cooking from the moment boiling starts, and boil shrimp just 2 minutes, no longer. Drain and remove shells; devein. Chill. Line cocktail glasses with lettuce, fill with shrimp and serve with Cocktail Sauce. Serves 4.

Cocktail Sauce:

1/2 cup tomato catsup
6 Tbsp. lemon or lime juice
1/8 tsp. salt

1 Tbsp. grated horseradish
3 drops Tabasco sauce
1/2 tsp. celery salt

Blend all ingredients; chill in refrigerator.

A seaside dinner of succulent Florida seafood and Key Lime Pie.

Pompano Amandine

Its delicate, especially fine-flavored flesh makes pompano Florida's "fish deluxe."

1–1¹/₂ lb. pompano
¹/₂ stick butter
¹/₄ tsp. salt

dash white pepper
2 Tbsp. slivered almonds
lime wedges and parsley

Clean pompano, but leave it whole, with the head on. Melt butter in small skillet, using enough to measure ¹/₄ inch deep in the pan. Saute fish until it flakes easily, 5–6 minutes on each side. Remove pompano to warmed serving dish; season with salt and pepper. In pan drippings, cook almonds until just pale golden. Pour butter-almond sauce over pompano. Garnish with lime and parsley. Serves 1.

"COCONUTTY" RECIPES

Coconut delicacies are as traditional to Key West as widow's walks and Martello Towers. Fresh coconut cake is a Key West trademark. It was served to President Truman, President Eisenhower, Secretary of State John Foster Dulles and countless other dignitaries who visited the island. Oldtimers insist that freshly grated coconut must be used. One meltingly-good taste and you will know how right they are! (Tip: Frozen grated coconut is the next best thing.)

Key West Coconut Cake

3/4 cup shortening	1 cup coconut milk
1 1/2 cup sugar	1 tsp. vanilla extract
3 cups cake flour	5 egg whites
4 tsp. baking powder	2 Tbsp. cooking oil
1/2 tsp. salt	

Cream together shortening and sugar. Sift together flour, baking powder and salt. Add alternately with coconut milk to creamed mixture. Add vanilla extract. Beat egg whites until stiff; fold into batter. Pour into 2 oiled 8- x 8- x 2-inch square layer pans or 2 oiled 9-inch layer pans. Bake in 375°F oven 30 minutes. Cool 5 minutes. Remove layers from pans; cool on wire rack. When cool, fill and frost. Makes 1 cake.

Coconut Filling:

2 egg whites	1 Tbsp. white corn syrup
1 1/2 cups sugar	1/2 tsp. salt
1/2 cup coconut milk	1 tsp. vanilla extract
	1 coconut, grated

Combine all ingredients except vanilla and coconut. With electric mixer, beat at high speed about 1 minute to blend. Then place over rapidly boiling water, using mixer to beat continuously until firm peaks form, about 8 minutes. Remove from heat, turn into bowl and add vanilla extract. Fill and frost cooled cake layers, sprinkling generously with grated coconut.

Coconut Cookie Balls

2 egg whites	2 cups grated coconut
1 cup sugar	1 tsp. vanilla extract
1 Tbsp. flour	

Beat egg whites until stiff. Beat in sugar, a little at a time; then beat in flour. Blend in coconut and vanilla. Drop by teaspoons onto well-greased cookie sheet. Bake in 350°F oven about 18 minutes or until lightly browned. Remove from pan at once. Makes about 30 cookies.

Queen of All Puddings

The British influence is evident in this rich pudding, brought to Key West from the Bahama Islands.

1 quart milk, scalded
2 cups soft bread crumbs
3 egg yolks
3/4 cup sugar
2 Tbsp. butter

1/2 cup guava jelly
3 egg whites
6 Tbsp. sugar
flaked coconut

Pour scalded milk over bread crumbs; cool. Beat egg yolks lightly with 3/4 cup sugar, add to milk and bread crumbs. Melt butter in a deep baking dish. Add butter to custard, then pour custard into baking dish. Preheat oven to 350°F; place pudding in oven in pan of warm water. Bake 1 hour 15 minutes, or until silver knife inserted in center comes out clean. When pudding has set, remove from oven and spread top with guava jelly. Beat egg whites until foamy, gradually adding sugar until peaks form. Swirl on top; sprinkle with coconut. Bake in 350°F oven 12–15 minutes, until lightly browned. Serves 4–6.

Coconut Chicken Salad

1 cup chopped cooked chicken
1 cup diced celery
1/2 cup grated coconut
1/2 cup green seedless grapes
1/4 cup chopped pecans or walnuts

salt to taste
1/2 cup mayonnaise, thinned
    with a little cream
1 ripe avocado
1 lime

Prepare chicken, celery, coconut, grapes, nuts. Combine. Add salt; mix with mayonnaise. Chill. Cut avocado in half; rub lime on front to prevent darkening. When ready to serve, fill avocado halves with chicken salad. Serves 2.

OTHER TROPICAL FRUIT RECIPES

The Original Key Lime Pie

The Key Lime Pie originated by pioneer settlers of the Florida Keys has gained worldwide recognition. Here is the original recipe, plus two delicious variations.

6 egg yolks, beaten slightly
1 15-oz. can sweetened condensed milk
1/2 cup Key Lime juice (or Persian lime)

1 9-inch baked pie shell, pastry or crumb
6 egg whites, stiffly beaten
4 Tbsp. sugar

Combine egg yolks and condensed milk. Mix well. Add lime juice; blend well. Turn into baked pie shell. Beat egg whites until stiff peaks form, gradually adding sugar. Swirl onto pie, spreading to edge of pie shell all around. Bake in 300°F oven until meringue is pale honey-colored.

Frozen Lime Pie

1/2 cup Key Lime or Persian Lime juice
1 15-oz. can sweetened condensed milk
5 egg whites
2 Tbsp. sugar

1 Tbsp. grated lemon rind
few drops green food color
1 9-inch graham cracker pie shell

Combine lime juice and condensed milk, stirring until thick and smooth. Beat egg whites until foamy. Add sugar, one tablespoon at a time, and continue beating until stiff. Add food color. Fold in lime-milk mixture. Sprinkle lemon rind on bottom of pie shell; turn filling into shell. Chill until set. Freeze and keep until time to serve, or serve without freezing. For topping, swirl on sweetened whipped cream. (For instructions, see Whipped Cream Frosting, page 55.)

LIME SOUR

This potent mixture is a great favorite on the Florida Keys. Natives like it on seafood cocktail, seafood salad, or broiled, baked or fried fish:
Strain 1 cup Key Lime juice into a bottle. Add 1 tablespoon salt and cork tightly. Let stand at room temperature until fermented—two to four weeks.

A pirate parrot watches over gold doubloons and Lime Chiffon Pie.

Lime Chiffon Pie

1 envelope unflavored gelatin
1/4 cup cold water
3 eggs, separated
1 cup sugar, divided
1/2 cup lime juice

1/4 tsp. salt
green food coloring
1 tsp. grated lemon peel
1 cup heavy cream, whipped
1 baked 9-inch pie shell

Soften gelatin in cold water. In top of double boiler, beat egg yolks slightly. Add 2/3 cup sugar, lime juice and salt. Cook over hot water until thick, stirring constantly; remove from heat. Stir in softened gelatin until thoroughly dissolved. Tint pale green with food coloring. Chill until slightly thickened. Beat egg whites until stiff but not dry. Gradually beat in remaining 1/3 cup sugar and grated lemon peel. Fold into gelatin mixture, then fold in half of whipped cream. Pile into cooled pie shell; chill until firm. Swirl remaining whipped cream onto top of pie. Refrigerate until ready to serve.

Guacamole

*Tip: If guacamole must stand for some time, put it in the
refrigerator with an avocado pit in the center and it will not darken.*

2 ripe avocados
juice of 1 lime
1/2 tsp. salt
1/2 tsp. chili powder

2 tsp. fresh onion juice
4 drops red hot sauce
1/2 of 3-oz. package cream cheese
1 Tbsp. minced pimiento (optional)

Peel avocados, remove pits and mash with silver fork to prevent darkening. Add lime juice, then blend in seasonings and cream cheese. If pimiento is used, stir it in last. Use as a dip with potato chips, or stuff tomatoes for salad.

Caribbean Guava Punch

2 quarts Jamaican rum
1 1/2 cups Key Lime juice
2 1/4 lbs. sugar
2 quarts strong tea
1 quart sweet sherry

2 quarts water
1 lb. guava jelly
1/2 pint brandy
3 quarts ginger ale

Mix all ingredients in large punch bowl, well iced. Just before serving time, add ginger ale.

Tropical Dessert Sauce

A sauce in the Keys tradition, great over Jell-o or ice cream.

1 5-oz. can evaporated milk
2/3 cup sugar

1/2 tsp. almond extract
juice of 2 Key Limes

Chill milk; beat with electric mixer until foamy. Add sugar; whip again. Squeeze limes, strain juice. Add almond extract and juice. Tangy but sweet, this has the consistency of whipped cream. Makes 1 1/4 cups. ✤

4 Sunny Gulf Coast

Spanish pirates once rode the waves where now a peaceful sailboat regatta drifts across Tampa Bay off St. Petersburg.

Tampa is the name of the Indian town shown on 1580 maps. Fifty-two years before that, Narvaéz, commissioned governor of Florida, took a party of men inland to explore. He was followed in 1539 by deSoto, who came ashore and conquered the local Indians.

The first American settlement was a log fort built in 1823. By the time of the War Between the States, Tampa's vast pastures were filled with cattle and there was brisk trade with Cuba.

When four companies moved out to join the Confederate Army, the defenseless town was blockaded and shelled in 1863 and later occupied by Federal forces. The city was in desperate condition after the war when yellow fever swept through the area.

Progress did not really begin until 1889, when the railroad reached Tampa. Phosphate was discovered and a lively industry sprang up. Ybor brought his cigar factory and thousands of workers. And Henry Plant built the huge Tampa Bay Hotel, hoping to outdo Henry Flagler's east coast success. It became troop headquarters during the Spanish American War, and Colonel Theodore Roosevelt trained his Rough Riders in the hotel's backyard.

There was another great epidemic, this time of typhoid fever, and troops were tended by Clara Barton, founder of the Red Cross.

After the war's end, Tampa again thrived. It became the capital of the world for production of high class, handmade Havana cigars. The boom period saw hotels and apartments built, also the Gandy Bridge which spanned Tampa Bay and connected the city with St. Petersburg.

This fine natural port made it a natural spot for concentrated action during World War II, and shipbuilding gave jobs to thousands. Another aid to community growth was MacDill Air Force Base.

Tampa thrived until the mid-1900s when the tobacco embargo caused the industry to move to Central America. The historic 110-block area of cigar factories has come to life again, with deserted buildings converted to restaurants, art galleries and boutiques.

Tampa's airport, one of the nation's finest, is the destination of many tourists who then make the short drive to Disney World. It's worth the drive to see the spectacular Skyway Bridge linking Tampa and St. Petersburg with south Florida.

Each February, Tampa surrenders to fun when swashbuckling "pirates" reinvade the city via the world's only fully-rigged pirate ship during the annual Gasparilla Festival. This duplicates the invasion of José Gaspar, a nineteenth century buccaneer.

While Southern cooking holds first place among long-time Floridians, Spanish restaurants like the world-famous Columbia restaurant in Ybor City have spiced local menus with Latin flavor. Party fare is likely to feature garbanzo bean soup, arroz con pollo and fresh Dixie coconut cake.

Population has soared along the Gulf Coast. Sleepy little Marco Island is now studded with waterfront hotels. Naples, with luxury estates and upscale shopping, is becoming known as the Palm Beach of the west coast. And Sarasota, with its opera, ballet, artists' colony and circus history, is a haven for sun-seeking retirees.

The entire coast is a land of white sugar beaches strewn with beautiful seashells and lazy rivers that join streams with the blue Gulf—an ideal area for boating and fishing.

In 1905, 25 miles northwest of Tampa, Tarpon Springs was born. This Greek community was settled by sponge fishermen lured from their homeland to the bountiful west coast sponge beds.

In colorful ceremonies, the sponge fleet is blessed each January 6 and young men dive for the golden cross flung into the bay by the archbishop. Even more exciting is the Greek food—savory, herb-blessed lamb, sweet stone crab claws, and a salad that is a work of art.

Agriculture is big business, providing plenty of locally produced citrus and beef, garden vegetables, guavas, watermelons and berries. With seafood plentiful along the coast, local cooks do great things with shrimp and crabmeat, lobster and fish.

YBOR CITY SPECIALTIES

Tender-Crust Cuban Bread

1¹/₂ package active dry yeast
2²/₃ cups warm water
1¹/₄ Tbsp. salt
1¹/₄ Tbsp. sugar

8 cups sifted all-purpose flour
¹/₄ cup yellow corn meal
¹/₄ cup melted butter or margarine

Dissolve yeast in ²/₃ cups warm water until soft. Add salt, sugar and remaining 2 cups warm water, stirring thoroughly. Add flour a cup at a time, beating it in with a wooden spoon. Working on a lightly floured board, knead dough for about 15 minutes, until it is smooth and elastic. Place in a large, well-oiled bowl, brush top with melted butter and cover with a tea towel. Set in a warm place for about one hour, until dough doubles in size. Punch dough down with your fist. Again on lightly floured board, shape dough into two long, narrow loaves. Sprinkle cookie sheet with corn meal and place loaves on it. Cut several slashes in top. Let rise 5 minutes. Brush tops with melted butter and place in cold oven. Turn oven to 400°F and bake 45 minutes or until loaves are golden brown. Place pan of boiling water in oven during baking time. Remove bread from oven, and again brush it with melted butter. Makes 2 loaves, golden crusted outside, light and snowy inside.

Florida Mullet with Spanish Sauce

1 3-lb. mullet (or red snapper)
salt and pepper
flour
6 Tbsp. melted butter
¹/₄ cup chopped onion
2 cups chopped celery
¹/₄ cup chopped green pepper
3 cups canned tomatoes
1 tsp. Worcestershire sauce

1 Tbsp. catsup
¹/₂ tsp. chili powder
¹/₂ lemon, thinly sliced
1 bay leaf
1 clove minced garlic
1 tsp. salt
2 tsp. sugar
dash cayenne pepper

Mix flour, salt and pepper and coat mullet inside and out. Melt butter in skillet and over low heat, cook onion, celery and green pepper in butter for 15 minutes. Add all remaining ingredients and simmer until celery is tender. Press mixture through potato ricer; pour sauce over cleaned fish and bake in 350°F oven 45 minutes, basting frequently with Spanish sauce. Serves 4 generously.

Spanish Bean Soup
(from the famous Columbia Restaurant)

1/2 lb. dried garbanzo beans
10 cups water
1 Tbsp. salt
1 beef bone
1 ham bone
2 quarts water
1/4 lb. salt pork, chopped fine

pinch paprika
1 Tbsp. shortening
1 chopped onion
1 lb. potatoes, peeled and quartered
1 pinch saffron
*1 chorizo (Spanish sausage), cut
    in thin slices*

Place beans in salted water in a large pot, to soak overnight. Next day, drain water and place beans, beef and ham bones and 2 quarts water in a large pot. Place over low heat; simmer 45 minutes. Fry the chopped salt pork, add paprika and onion (plus 1 tablespoon shortening if needed) and cook until onion is tender. Add to beans, then add potatoes. Toast saffron on the cover of a casserole or in the oven and mash before measuring. Mix it with a little hot stock from the pot, then add it to the soup. Taste and season with salt and pepper. When the potatoes are done, put chorizo slices in the soup and serve it hot. Serves 4.

Chicken and Yellow Rice Valenciana

1 2 1/2-lb. frying chicken, quartered
1/2 cup fresh olive oil
2 chopped onions
1 chopped green pepper
1 clove garlic, chopped fine
2 Tbsp. salt
1 bay leaf
1 small can tomatoes, drained
1/4 tsp. pepper

2 1/2 cups rice
5 cups water
2 chicken bouillon cubes
1/2 cup sherry wine (optional)
1/8 tsp. saffron
1 cup green peas
1 dozen green olives
1 small can pimientos

Brown chicken in olive oil over medium heat. Remove chicken from pan. Add onions, green pepper and garlic. Continue cooking until slightly brown, about 5 minutes. Return chicken to pot and stir in salt, bay leaf, tomatoes and pepper. Add rice, water in which 2 chicken bouillon cubes have been dissolved, and wine. Dissolve saffron in small amount of water and add (or use a few drops of yellow food color mixed with water). Bring to a boil. Bake in preheated oven at 350°F for 20 minutes. Garnish with green peas, olives and pimientos. Serves 4.

Chicken and Rice Valenciana is an Ybor City Specialty

GREEK DISHES

Lamb Kebobs, Greek Style

$^1/_2$ tsp. Tabasco
$^1/_2$ cup olive or salad oil
$^1/_4$ cup lime or lemon juice
$^1/_4$ cup red wine, optional
1 Tbsp. onion juice
1 tsp. dry mustard
$^1/_2$ tsp. salt

$^1/_8$ tsp. basil
$^1/_8$ tsp. thyme
2 lbs. boneless lamb shoulder cut in
    $1^1/_2$-inch cubes
1 green pepper cut in 1 inch pieces
3 tomatoes, quartered
12 small whole onions

Blend Tabasco, oil, lime juice, wine and onion juice in bowl. Add dry mustard, salt, basil and thyme. Add meat cubes. (Beef chuck may be substituted, but if used should be sprinkled with meat tenderizer.) Let stand 5 hours or overnight in refrigerator. Alternate meat and vegetables on skewers. Place in preheated broiler or on grill about 4 inches from heat. Broil approximately 10 minutes on each side. Serve with rice pilaf. Serves 6.

Louis Pappas' Famous Greek Salad

Served at Louis Pappas Restaurant in Tarpon Springs, this is called a salad for 4.

1 large head lettuce
3 cups potato salad (see below)
12 sprigs watercress
2 tomatoes cut into 6 wedges each
1 peeled cucumber, cut into 8 long
    fingers
1 peeled avocado, cut into wedges
4 portions of Feta cheese
1 green pepper, cut into 8 rings
4 slices canned cooked beets

4 peeled, cooked shrimp
4 anchovy fillets
12 Greek black olives
4 radishes, cut like roses
4 whole green onions
1/2 cup distilled white vinegar
1/4 cup each olive and salad oil,
    blended
oregano

Potato salad:

6 boiled potatoes, sliced and cooled
2 medium onions, chopped
1/4 cup finely chopped parsley

salt to taste
1/2 cup thinly sliced green onion
1/2 cup salad dressing

Save 10 outside lettuce leaves and shred remaining lettuce finely. Prepare all vegetables as indicated above. Spread whole lettuce leaves on a platter. In the center, mound potato salad and cover it with shredded lettuce, then watercress. Alternate tomato wedges and cucumber fingers around outside of platter; circle with avocado slices. Atop the salad, arrange the slices of Feta cheese, green pepper slices, olives, peppers, and green onions. Finally, top the salad with beet slices, shrimp and anchovy fillets. Sprinkle with vinegar and blended oils, then with oregano. Serve at once with toasted Greek garlic bread.

Moussaka Potatoes with Beef

1/2 clove garlic, chopped
1/2 cup oil for frying, preferably olive oil
6–8 medium potatoes, sliced
1 large onion, chopped
1 lb. ground beef (or lamb)
1 tsp. salt
1/4 tsp. pepper

pinch cinnamon
pinch sugar
1 cup water
1/4 cup dry red wine
2 cans tomato sauce, heated
2 bay leaves

Lightly brown garlic in oil; remove. Saute potatoes in oil until light brown but not done. Set potatoes aside. Mix meat, onion, garlic, salt and pepper to taste. Fry for 3 minutes. Spread meat mixture between layers of potatoes in oiled baking dish, starting and ending with potatoes. Combine wine, water, tomato sauce, cinnamon and sugar. Place bay leaves atop casserole and pour over all the wine liquid. Bake in 350°F oven 45 to 60 minutes. Remove bay leaves before serving hot. Serves 6.

Greek Honey Cakes (Melomacarona)

2 cups salad oil
1/4 lb. butter
1/2 cup sugar
1/2 cup orange juice
5 cups sifted flour
3 tsp. baking powder
1/4 cup water

1 cup finely chopped walnuts
1/2 tsp. cinnamon
1/8 tsp. ground cloves
1/8 cup rum
1 lb. honey
1/4 cup warm water
1/2 cup finely chopped walnuts

Stir until blended oil, butter and sugar; stir in orange juice then flour and mix till smooth. Quickly mix baking powder with 1/4 cup water and stir at once into dough. Mix in 1 cup walnuts, cinnamon and cloves. Shape dough into cakes 3 x 1 1/2-inch. Bake on ungreased cookie sheet in 350°F oven 20 to 25 minutes. Cool on wire rack. Warm honey and mix with 1/4 cup warm water. Dip cool cakes into honey, sprinkle with chopped walnuts and drain on rack over waxed paper. Makes about 24.

TROPICAL FRUIT RECIPES

Hot Wine Orange Punch

juice of 1 orange
1 1/2 cups water

1/2 lb. sugar
1 bottle red wine

In one saucepan, heat water and half of juice squeezed from orange. In another pan, dissolve sugar with remaining juice. Combine; boil 10 minutes. Heat red wine till it bubbles; pour in the orange-sugar mixture. Serve hot with thin slices of orange floating on top. A stimulating cold weather drink! Serves 6.

Dixie Coconut Cake

Coconut is baked in the cake layers and used in frosting.

3 cups sifted cake flour
2 tsp. double-acting baking powder
1/2 tsp. salt
1/2 cup butter
1 1/2 cups sugar

1 cup shredded coconut
1 cup water
1 1/2 tsp. lemon extract
4 egg whites, stiffly beaten

Sift flour once, measure, add baking powder and salt; sift twice more. Cream butter until smooth, gradually adding sugar and creaming until soft and fluffy To this, add coconut, then flour, then water, a little each time, beating well after each addition. When batter is smooth, stir in lemon extract; fold in egg whites which should be quite stiff. Bake in 2 greased loaf pans 8- x 4- x 3-inches at 350°F for 1 hour and 15 minutes. Frost top and sides with Coconut Seven-Minute Frosting (see page 54).

Coconut Seven-Minute Frosting

2 unbeaten egg whites
1¹/₂ cups sugar
5 Tbsp. cold water

1¹/₂ tsp. light corn syrup
1 tsp. vanilla
1 cup lightly toasted coconut

In upper double boiler, combine egg whites, sugar, water and corn syrup; beat with rotary egg beater until well mixed. Place over rapidly boiling water and continue beating. Cook 7 minutes or until frosting stands in peaks. Remove from heat, add vanilla, beat until thick. Spread on cake, and sprinkle with toasted coconut. Makes enough to frost a two-layer cake, including top and sides.

Pineapple Drop Cookies

1 cup light brown sugar
¹/₂ cup shortening mixed with butter
1 unbeaten egg
1 tsp. vanilla
³/₄ cup crushed pineapple
2 cups sifted all-purpose flour

1 tsp. baking powder
¹/₂ tsp. salt
¹/₂ tsp. baking soda
³/₄ cup chopped walnuts
¹/₂ cup raisins

Heat oven to 375°F. Stir together sugar, shortening, egg and vanilla till blended. Spoon pineapple from can with as little syrup as possible into measuring cup and add. Stir in sifted dry ingredients, then walnuts and raisins. Drop by heaping teaspoonfuls on ungreased cookie sheet. Bake at 375°F for 12 minutes till lightly browned. Makes 36.

Florida Fruit Cake

1 cup salad oil
1¹/₂ cups brown sugar
4 eggs
3 cups sifted flour
1 tsp. baking powder
2 tsp. salt
1 tsp. cloves

1 cup orange juice
1 cup chopped candied pineapple
2 cups candied cherries, halved
1¹/₂ cups seedless raisins
1 cup chopped dates
2 Tbsp. peach brandy

In large bowl, beat oil, sugar and eggs 2 minutes. Sift together 2 cups flour with baking powder, salt and spices. Stir into oil mixture with orange juice. Mix remaining cup of flour with fruits and nuts. Combine with batter and mix thoroughly. Pour batter into two 9- x 5-inch loaf pans lined with greased brown paper. Bake in 275°F oven 2¹/₂–3 hours. Remove and cool. Sprinkle brandy over cake, wrap and store in cool place. Decorate with candied pineapple and cherries. Makes 2 loaves.

Lime Pudding Cake

This dessert has crusty cake topping above, rich lime sauce beneath.

2 eggs, separated
3/4 cup sugar, divided
3 Tbsp. lime juice
1 tsp. grated lime rind

3 Tbsp. flour
1/4 tsp. salt
1 cup milk

Beat egg whites, gradually adding 1/2 cup sugar, until stiff and glossy. Set aside. Beat egg yolks. Add lime juice and grated rind to egg yolks. Mix 1/4 cup sugar, flour and salt together. Sprinkle over lime mixture and beat well. Add milk; blend well. Fold egg yolk mixture into beaten egg whites. Pour into 6 greased custard cups. Set in shallow pan of water and bake in 350°F oven 35 minutes until firm. Serves 6.

Orange-Rum Cream Cake

1 3/4 cups sifted cake flour
1 tablespoon baking powder
1/4 tsp. salt
1/2 cup shortening

1 cup sugar
8 beaten egg yolks
1 tsp. grated orange rind
1/2 cup milk

Have all ingredients at room temperature. Sift together twice flour, baking powder and salt. Cream shortening till fluffy; gradually add sugar. Blend till mixture is creamy. Stir in egg yolks and orange rind until well mixed. Alternately add dry ingredients and milk, beating after each addition. Turn into two greased 8-inch cake pans and bake in 350°F oven 30 minutes. Cool 10 minutes; turn onto cake rack. Fill with Orange-Rum Filling and frost with Whipped Cream Frosting.

Orange-Rum Filling:

3 Tbsp. butter
3/4 tsp. grated orange rind
1 1/2 cup sifted confectioners' sugar, divided

dash salt
2 Tbsp. orange juice
1 tsp. rum

Cream butter with orange rind. Gradually add 1/2 cup sugar, blending after each addition. Add salt; mix well. Add remaining sugar alternately with orange juice, beating till smooth after each addition. Blend in rum. Spread on cake layer.

Whipped Cream Frosting:

1 cup heavy cream
1/2 tsp. vanilla
3 Tbsp. sifted confectioners' sugar

Whip heavy cream until stiff. Fold in vanilla and confectioners' sugar. Spread over cooled cake. ✖

SWEET THINGS

Marshmallow Fudge Cake

A novel filling and so easy to do!

2²/₃ cups sifted cake flour
3¹/₂ tsp. baking powder
¹/₂ tsp. salt
2 cups sugar
¹/₃ cup salad oil

2 eggs
1 cup milk
1 tsp. vanilla
2 oz. unsweetened chocolate, melted
16 marshmallows

Sift together twice flour, baking powder, salt and sugar. Add oil, eggs, milk, vanilla and chocolate; blend well then beat 2 minutes. Pour into two 8-inch square pans, greased and lined with waxed paper. Bake in 325°F oven 1 hour. Cool. Place marshmallows atop one layer and broil to lightly brown. Cool 15 minutes. Top with plain cake layer and cover with fudge frosting.

Quick Caramel Cake

A tasty version with baked-on topping.

2 cups cake flour
3 tsp. baking powder
1 tsp. salt
1¹/₄ cups sugar

¹/₂ cup shortening
³/₄ cup milk
1¹/₂ tsp. vanilla
2 eggs

Topping:
2 egg whites
1 cup brown sugar
¹/₂ cup chopped pecans

Let all ingredients stand at room temperature 45 minutes before use. To sifted flour, add baking powder, salt, sugar; sift again into large mixer bowl. Add shortening, milk, vanilla. Beat 2 minutes with mixer at low speed. Add unbeaten eggs and beat 1 minute longer. Pour into greased 8¹/₂- x 13¹/₂-inch pan. Set aside. Clean mixer beaters and beat egg whites till stiff but not dry. Gradually add brown sugar; beat well. Spread atop cake; sprinkle with nuts and bake on center rack in 350°F oven 35 minutes. Makes 1 cake. ✤

5 The Heartland

Spanish explorers never found gold in Florida,
but they brought citrus—Florida's richest treasure.

Just a few hours by car takes you far from the glamour of the Gold Coast into Florida's quietly beautiful heartland, a world of beef cattle ranches, orange groves and vegetable farms. To the north in Ocala, racing thoroughbreds are raised on the rolling green hills. History is being made in the area near Orlando, where Disney World opened its gates in 1971, a fabulous entertainment theme park and resort drawing families and children both young and old from all parts of the world.

Around Lake Okeechobee, rich black mucklands have been producing sugar cane in volume since 1929. The industry, centered in Clewiston, became a giant when Castro's Cuba was cut out of the American market and Florida sugar cane became a prime supplier of the nation's needs.

In this same region and on farms far down in Homestead south of Miami, about 90 percent of the nation's supply of winter vegetables grows. Two large Seminole Indian Reservations are near the lake—Big Cypress 30 miles east of

Immokalee and Brighton—35,660 acres on the northwest shore of Lake Okeechobee.

The Indians are hardworking cowboys whose herds of beef cattle are steadily being improved. But other ranchers account for most of the more than 75 percent of Florida's beef cattle which are produced in central and south central areas, especially in Polk, Osceola, Hendry, Highlands, Hardee, DeSoto, Hillsborough, Okeechobee and Glades counties.

From Punta Gorda to Kissimmee, cattle graze on the flat prairies. Levis, ten-gallon hats and boots are the uniform of the day and rodeos feature exciting riding and roping in the true western tradition.

Kissimmee called Cow Town — had the dubious honor of originating the first bar for drinking men who did not want to get off their horses to drink. The ride-in bar was begun about 1870, ten years before the west adopted the idea.

Spanish explorers brought cattle into the state and their runaways turned wild, then were herded by the Indians. During the second Spanish occupation of Florida, from 1813 to 1821, the Spanish gave land grants to homesteaders who stocked the ranges with cattle from Europe as well as herds driven down from the southern states. As the Seminoles retreated into the Everglades, cattle ranchers moved in behind them all along the Kissimmee Valley.

White "humpbacked" Brahman cows were introduced because of their hardiness, resistance to insects, disease, heat, and the ability to live off sparse grasslands. They were improved by crossbreeding with Black Angus, Hereford, Santa Gertrudis and others, but the trend is now toward more purebred cattle other than the Brahman, because ranchers are improving their pastures.

By 1895, when Frederic Remington, the noted writer-painter, visited Florida, he described the Cracker cowboys as a wild-looking group with "long hair, broad-brimmed hat, and gun slung on hip." The wild west was no wilder than Florida in the nineteenth century. Cattle rustling was widespread; shootouts and stabbings were common. Ranchers did not venture out at night nor enter woods alone in some areas. Criminals would attack then flee deep into the Everglades' watery wilderness to hide. At last, outraged citizens called a halt and law and order were reestablished.

Throughout the heartland, steak and chops restaurants are popular. And the cowboys' campfire victuals are much enjoyed: fried white bacon, grits, beans, biscuits or cold corn pone, coffee boiled with the grounds until it is strong and black.

Moving north in the state, one enters a land that flows into gently rolling hills, dipping down to incredibly blue lakes. Ironically, the Spanish who failed in their search for Florida gold, brought into the state the citrus seeds that were to produce its greatest treasure—oranges, grapefruit, lemons and tangerines.

Because citrus was found to have medicinal value, Columbus was under orders to carry with him seeds of the first citrus trees to reach the New World. Scattered throughout the Antilles, orange trees flourished and covered some Caribbean islands.

There are strong indications that Ponce de Leon introduced oranges to the North American mainland when he discovered Florida in 1513.

Later in 1539, Hernando de Soto planted more trees during his expedition to Florida. Spanish law required that each sailor bound for America carry one hundred seeds but because the seeds dried out, young trees were later substituted. Seminole Indians carried oranges into the Florida wilderness and today, sour orange trees thrive deep in the Everglades!

In the '90s orange grove acreage dropped to 791,000 acres, a decrease caused in the 1980s when four severe freezes destroyed many groves in the northern tier of citrus country. However, Florida still produces 70% of all citrus grown in the U.S. each year. And since 1950, frozen concentrate of citrus juices has been a major industry.

Already the fun capital of Florida, with 30,000 acres occupied by the Magic Kingdom, Epcot and MGM Studios, hotels, campgrounds and nightclubs, Disney World continues to grow. Yet to come are more thrill rides, exotic landscapes and wildlife areas, as well as a community of homes.

Central Florida is a land still rich in deer, quail, doves and other game. Truck lands produce fine beans, cabbage, tomatoes, peas, cucumbers, lettuce. Honey is plentiful, as are poultry and beef, milk and eggs.

While the Disney resort hotels, especially the Epcot restaurants, feature international fare that pleases visitors, still in the heartland homes, traditional Southern food continues as popular as it was a hundred years ago.

CLEWISTON FISH FRY

Sugar is the big industry in Clewiston, and sweet-meated freshwater catfish from Lake Okeechobee hot from the frying pan, accompanied by crusty hush puppies, are the favorite foods at lakeside barbecues.

Fried Catfish

2 pounds skinned, pan-dressed catfish
1 beaten egg
2 Tbsp. milk
1 cup white cornmeal

2 tsp. salt
oil for deep frying
parsley
lemon slices

Clean and wash catfish. Dry on absorbent paper. Combine egg and milk in one bowl, cornmeal and salt in another. Dip fish into egg mixture then into cornmeal mixture. Heat oil to 350°F and fry fish until golden brown, about 8 minutes. Drain on absorbent paper. Garnish with parsley and lemon. Serve with hot hush puppies. Serves 4.

Hush Puppies

Old-timers say the name originated around the campfire when hunters tossed the hounds these hot breads to keep them quiet.

2 cups cornmeal
1 tablespoon flour
2 tsp. baking powder
1/2 tsp. salt
1 well beaten egg

3/4 cup water
1 small onion, chopped fine
bacon drippings, or oil in which
    fish was fried

Sift together cornmeal, flour, baking powder and salt. Mix egg, water and onion in bowl. Combine with dry ingredients and drop from a spoon into 380°F fat, dipping spoon first into hot fat, then into batter. Fry 6 or more at a time until crisp and golden (about 1 minute), lift with slotted spoon and drain on paper towels. Serve hot with fish, or cook bite-size and serve as appetizers with beverages. Makes 20.

Corn Fritters

1 cup corn, drained
2 slightly beaten eggs
1/3 cup flour
1/2 tsp. baking powder

1 tsp. salt
1/8 tsp. pepper
2 Tbsp. salad oil

Mix corn with slightly beaten eggs. Sift together flour, baking powder, salt and pepper. Combine corn and flour mixtures. Heat oil medium hot and drop fritter batter into oil. Fry until brown on bottom, turn and brown other side. Serve hot. Makes about 10. (If so desired, these may be sprinkled with a little confectioners' sugar and served as appetizers.)

This holiday fruit compote is laced with spices and wine.

FLORIDA CITRUS RECIPES

Christmas Citrus Compote

4 Florida oranges
1 papaya, fresh or canned
1 pineapple, fresh or canned
2¹/₂ cups halved, seedless red and
    green grapes (about ¹/₂ lb.)

1 cup Marsala wine
1 cup water
³/₄ cup sugar
1 stick cinnamon
3 whole cloves

Cut 3 strips orange peel from 1 orange, using vegetable peeler; reserve.
Peel oranges and cut into crosswise slices. Pare papaya, cut in half lengthwise
and remove seeds; cut into cubes. To prepare pineapple, cut off stem and
crown ends. Cut off rind all around, from top to bottom; remove eyes with
pointed knife. Cut into quarters lengthwise. Cut away core. Cut remaining meat
into fingers about 2 inches long. Combine oranges, papaya, pineapple and
grapes in large bowl. Combine wine, water, sugar, cinnamon stick, cloves and
orange peel in saucepan; stir over medium heat until sugar dissolves. Reduce
heat and simmer 5 minutes. Remove spices and orange peel. Cool to luke-
warm. Pour syrup over fruit in bowl; cover and refrigerate 6 hours or
overnight. Serves 12.

Fruit Salad with Orange Cream Salad Dressing

1 egg	1½ Tbsp. fresh lemon juice
3 Tbsp. sugar	¼ cup heavy cream, whipped
¼ tsp. salt	FRUITS FOR SALAD: fresh orange and
¼ tsp. ginger	grapefruit sections, pitted grapes,
2 tsp. butter	pineapple chunks
½ cup fresh orange juice	crisp salad greens

Beat egg in top of double boiler. Add sugar, salt, ginger, butter, orange juice and lemon juice; mix well. Place over boiling water and cook, stirring constantly, until mixture thickens slightly, 5 to 7 minutes. Chill. Just before serving, fold in whipped cream. Arrange fresh fruit on crisp greens; serve with dressing. Makes 1 cup of dressing, enough for 6 servings.

Grapefruit Cole Slaw

2 Florida grapefruit	½ tsp. salt
3 cups shredded cabbage	2 tsp. sugar
⅓ cup mayonnaise	½ tsp. celery seed

Chill grapefruit. Cut off peel in strips from top to bottom, slicing deep enough to remove white membrane. Then cut out sections from top to bottom, removing any remaining membrane. Place sections in bowl with cabbage. Combine remaining ingredients; add to cabbage. Toss lightly. Serves 6.

Baked Stuffed Pork Chops

8 1-inch rib or loin pork chops	3 cups stale ¼-inch bread cubes
salt, pepper	3 Tbsp. minced onion
2 Tbsp. oil	¾ tsp. salt
1 cup finely diced celery	½ tsp. Tabasco
1 6-oz. can frozen Florida grapefruit	⅓ cup brown sugar
concentrate, thawed and divided	

Sprinkle pork chops with salt and pepper. Brown in oil in skillet until golden brown on both sides, 15 to 20 minutes. Remove pork chops, saving 4 tablespoons of pan oil. Combine celery, ¼ cup grapefruit juice concentrate and pan oil; cook over medium heat 2 minutes. Add bread cubes, onion, salt, Tabasco; mix thoroughly. Combine remaining ½ cup grapefruit juice concentrate and brown sugar. Pour over pork chops in casserole. Arrange stuffing on top of pork chops. Bake, covered, in 350°F oven 30 minutes; remove cover and bake 15 minutes longer or until chops are tender. Serves 8.

Orange Sweet Potato Cups

3 lbs. sweet potatoes
3 Tbsp. melted butter
1/2 cup sugar
1 tsp. salt
1 tsp. vanilla

2 tsp. grated orange rind
1/3 cup orange juice
3 Temple or Navel oranges
1 cup mini-marshmallows

Boil sweet potatoes until tender; remove skins, mash and mix with all ingredients except oranges and marshmallows. Cut oranges in half crosswise; remove all juice and pulp, but keep rind whole. Fill with hot sweet potato mixture. Place in greased baking pan and bake 30 minutes at 350°F. Garnish with marshmallows and return to oven to brown. Serves 6.

Grapefruit-Avocado Salad

4 small heads Bibb lettuce
1 large grapefruit, peeled and
    sectioned
1 medium avocado, sliced lengthwise

1 large purple onion, sliced thin
1 cup pineapple chunks
tart French dressing

Chill all ingredients. Carefully trim out lettuce core so that the head will sit flat. For each serving, place washed lettuce on a plate and tuck into the leaves grapefruit sections, avocado slices, onion and pineapple chunks. Serve with tart French dressing. Serves 4.

Molasses-Orange Bread

1/2 cup sugar
22/3 cups sifted all-purpose flour
1/2 tsp. baking soda
2 tsp. baking powder
11/2 tsp. salt
1 cup coarsely chopped pecans

2/3 cup evaporated milk
1 Tbsp. grated orange rind
1/2 cup orange juice
2 Tbsp. salad oil
1/2 cup unsulphured molasses

Sift together sugar, flour, baking soda, baking powder and salt; add nuts. Combine evaporated milk, orange rind, orange juice, salad oil and molasses. Add to flour mixture all at once; stir just to blend. Turn into a well-greased loaf pan 9 x 5 x 3 inches. Bake in 325°F oven 1 hour 15 minutes. Cool before removing from pan. Makes 1 loaf.

Orange Meringue Pie

³/₄ cup sugar	1 Tbsp. grated orange rind
¹/₄ cup cornstarch	1 Tbsp. butter
¹/₈ tsp. salt	3 egg whites
1 cup orange juice	¹/₄ tsp. salt
¹/₂ cup water	6 Tbsp. sugar
1 Tbsp. lemon juice	Baked 9-inch pie shell
3 egg yolks, slightly beaten	

Combine sugar, cornstarch and salt in medium saucepan; slowly blend in orange juice, water and lemon juice. Cook and stir over medium heat until mixture is thickened and clear. Slowly stir a little of the hot mixture into egg yolks; add to remaining mixture. Blend in orange rind and butter; mix well. Cool thoroughly. Spoon into cooled pie shell.

Beat egg whites with salt until frothy. Add sugar gradually, beating well after each addition. Continue to beat until stiff peaks form. With a spoon, place mounds of meringue over pie filling, spreading to cover filling completely to edge of crust. Bake in 350°F oven 12 to 15 minutes. Cool thoroughly.

Orange Pecan Refrigerator Cookies

¹/₂ cup butter	3 cups flour, sifted
1 cup sugar	¹/₄ cup orange juice
¹/₄ tsp. salt	1¹/₂ cups pecan halves
1 tsp. grated orange rind	1 egg white
1 egg, slightly beaten	sugar
3 tsp. baking powder	

In one bowl, cream together butter, sugar and salt until light and fluffy; add orange rind and egg. Beat thoroughly. In another bowl, place baking powder and flour; sift together twice. To the creamed butter mixture add first the flour mixture, then the orange juice in 3 additions, stirring each time until well blended. Roll in wax paper and store in refrigerator overnight to chill thoroughly. Slice thin, keeping any unused dough in refrigerator as cookies bake. Place slices on an oiled cookie sheet; press a pecan half into the top of each cookie and then brush it with unbeaten egg white. Sprinkle with sugar. Bake in 375°F oven 10 to 12 minutes, until lightly browned. Cool on racks; store in air-tight cookie jar. Makes about 60.

Orange Juice Cake Surprise

1 large orange
1/2 cup sugar
1 cup raisins
3/4 cup chopped walnuts
1 cup sugar
1/2 cup margarine

2 unbeaten eggs
1 tsp. vanilla
2 cups sifted all-purpose flour
1 tsp. baking soda
1/2 tsp. salt
3/4 cup buttermilk

Squeeze juice from orange; add 1/2 cup sugar, stir and set aside. Run orange peel and raisins through fine blade of food processor; add nuts and set aside.

Using mixer, beat margarine and add 1 cup sugar, a little at a time. Beat in eggs, one at a time. Add vanilla. Sift together twice the flour, baking soda and salt; add this alternately with buttermilk in four additions, beating smooth after each. Stir in fruit and walnuts. Turn into greased 9- x 9- x 2-inch pan. Bake in 350°F oven about 45 minutes. Cool cake in pan 5 minutes, then pour orange juice mixture over it and wait 1 hour before serving warm as pudding, cold as refrigerator cake.

Feathery Lemon-Cheese Cake

The old-fashioned filling in this cake has no cheese in it, but its flavor and texture resemble cheese.

1 cup butter
2 cups sugar
4 eggs
3 cups sifted flour
3 tsp. baking powder

1/2 tsp. salt
1 cup milk
1/2 tsp. vanilla
1/2 tsp. lemon flavoring

Cream butter and sugar. Add one whole egg at a time, beating after each. Beat about 1 minute after all eggs have been added. Sift together dry ingredients twice. Add dry ingredients to creamed mixture, alternately with milk. Stir in vanilla and lemon flavoring. Grease and flour three 9-inch round cake pans. Pour batter into pans and bake in 350°F oven 40 minutes or until done. When cool, fill with Lemon-Cheese Filling. Cake may be sprinkled with confectioners' sugar or frosted with seven-minute frosting (see page 54). Or, a double amount of filling may be made, the whole cake frosted and filled with the lemon-cheese mixture.

Lemon-Cheese Filling:

1 cup sugar
4 Tbsp. cornstarch, dissolved
    in a little water
juice of 2 lemons

3 Tbsp. butter
2 eggs
2 egg yolks

Combine all ingredients and cook over hot water in double boiler, stirring constantly, until thick. Cool before spreading between layers.

Heavenly Cream Ambrosia

True traditional Southern ambrosia is simply orange sections tossed with freshly grated coconut and a bit of sugar. Marvelous though it is, this recipe is even more so.

1 cup heavy cream, whipped
1/2 cup sour cream
1 Tbsp. orange liqueur
2 cups orange sections

1 cup grapefruit sections
1 cup freshly grated coconut
1 cup miniature marshmallows

Whip cream then fold in sour cream and orange liqueur. Dice orange sections and grapefruit. Fold into cream with coconut and marshmallows. Cover and chill overnight. Garnish with sliced orange steeped in orange liqueur. Serves 8.

Tropicali Punch

1 6-oz. can frozen limeade concentrate
2 6-oz. cans frozen pineapple juice
   concentrate
1 6-oz. can frozen orange juice
   concentrate
13 6-oz. cans (9³/₄ cups) water

2 cups superfine sugar
3 12-oz. bottles cold ginger ale
Maraschino cherries
fresh orange dices
mint sprigs

Thaw all concentrates; add sugar and water, stirring until all sugar dissolves. Just before serving, place ice in large punch bowl; pour juices over ice. Add ginger ale, cherries, orange slices. Serve in glasses with mint sprig. (Orange sherbet may be used in bowl instead of ice, if desired.) Serves 30.

Iced Tea Punch

2 Tbsp. loose tea
2 cups boiling water
1 cup granulated sugar

1 cup orange juice
1/2 cup lemon juice
1 12-oz. bottle cold ginger ale

Pour boiling water over tea and let stand 5 minutes. Strain tea into pitcher. Add sugar; stir until dissolved. Pour in juices and chill. To serve, pour over ice in punch bowl and add ginger ale. Makes 10 cups.

Citrus Kiwi Compote

2 oranges, peeled, seeded, sectioned
2 pink grapefruit, peeled, seeded,
   sectioned
1 8-oz. can pineapple chunks,
   undrained

4 kiwifruit, peeled and thinly sliced
2 limes
1/2 cup apple juice
3 Tbsp. sugar
1/2 gallon orange sherbet

In a large bowl, combine oranges, grapefruit, pineapple and kiwifruit. Cut one lime in half. Slice one of the halves thinly and place in bowl with the fruit. Squeeze remaining 11/2 limes, strain the juice and add it to the fruit mixture. Stir in apple juice. Sprinkle with sugar. Cover and refrigerate several hours. Spoon fruit into dessert dishes and top with orange sherbet. Serves 8.

BEEF RECIPES

Tea-Marinated Florida Beef Roast

Statewide winner in Florida Beef Council contest!

Brown a 3- to 5-lb. Florida chuck or shoulder cut beef roast in 2 to 3 table-spoons oil. Make enough very strong tea to cover the roast 3/4 way. Simmer 3 to 5 hours, until meat is fork tender. Drain off tea and place meat in baking dish. Pour half of the following sauce over the meat. Bake uncovered at 325°F for 45 minutes, basting several times during baking.

<u>Sauce:</u>

1 cup chili sauce	2 Tbsp. bacon drippings
3 Tbsp. brown sugar	1 cup. water
juice of 2 lemons	1 tsp. paprika
1 Tbsp. Worcestershire sauce	3 Tbsp. vinegar
1/4 tsp. celery salt	1 tsp. salt
1/3 cup grated onion	

Combine all ingredients and stir to blend. Heat reserved sauce and serve it with the meat.

Beef Corn-Pone Pie

1 lb. ground beef	1 20-oz. can tomatoes
1 medium onion, chopped	1 20-oz. can kidney beans
1 medium green pepper, thinly sliced	salt
3 Tbsp. salad oil	1 tsp. chili powder (or to taste)

Cook onion and pepper in hot oil until onion is transparent but not brown Add beef; cook until lightly browned. Stir in remaining ingredients; let simmer. Add chili powder just before topping with cornbread mixture:

<u>Cornbread:</u>

1 1/2 cups cornmeal	2 cups buttermilk
3 Tbsp. flour	1 beaten egg
1 tsp. salt	2 Tbsp. bacon drippings, butter or
1 tsp. baking soda	margarine

Mix and sift dry ingredients. Add buttermilk and egg, stirring until well blended. Heat fat in skillet and add to batter. Turn beef mixture into iron fry-ing pan. Mix batter well, pour over beef mixture and bake in 450°F oven about 25 minutes, or until golden brown. Serves 6.

Barbecue Beef Loaf

2 lbs. ground beef
3/4 cup milk
1 1/2 cups soft bread crumbs
2 tsp. salt
1/8 tsp. pepper
1 medium carrot, grated

1/4 cup diced onion
2 beaten eggs
1/4 cup catsup
3 Tbsp. brown sugar
2 Tbsp. prepared mustard

Pour milk over bread crumbs. Add ground beef, salt, pepper, carrot, onion and beaten eggs. Mix thoroughly. Pack into 5- x 9-inch loaf pan. Mix together catsup, brown sugar, mustard, and spread on loaf. Bake in 300°F oven about 1 1/2 hours, or until brown and done. Serves 8.

Flank Steak Rolls

2 lbs. flank steak, cut in half
1 lb. mild sausage
1/4 tsp. basil
1/2 tsp. thyme
3 Tbsp. bacon drippings
1 28-oz. can tomatoes
1 6-oz. can tomato paste

1 large onion, chopped
3 tsp. salt
1/4 tsp. pepper
1 1/2 tsp. chili powder
1/2 clove garlic
1 12-oz. package wide noodles
butter or margarine

Have butcher cut meat to half thickness. Pound steak, sprinkle with basil and thyme then spread with sausage. Roll and tie with string. Brown in hot drippings; add all remaining ingredients except noodles and butter. Cover; bring to a boil then reduce to simmer and cook slowly 1 1/2 hours, or until meat is tender. Remove garlic. Cook noodles, drain, then place a large wedge of butter in the hot pan and turn noodles in butter until well coated. Remove string from steak roll and slice one inch thick. Serve meat with sauce atop hot noodles. Serves 6 generously.

Pioneer Pot Roast

1/4 lb. salt pork
salt and pepper
4-lb. chuck roast of beef
1 clove garlic, minced
flour

4 Tbsp. cooking oil
2 sliced onions
1 bay leaf
1 cup boiling water
1 Tbsp. Worcestershire sauce

Slice salt pork thinly and sprinkle with pepper. Slash roast deeply and insert pork slices. Rub roast with garlic and salt; dredge with flour. Heat oil and brown meat well. Place in large heavy pot, place onion and bay leaf on meat and pour in boiling water, and Worcestershire sauce. Bring to boil then reduce to simmer; cover and simmer 3 hours or until meat is tender. Add more water if needed. Serves 8.

Mom's Swiss Steak

1½ lbs. round steak, 1½ inches thick
1 tsp. salt
¼ tsp. pepper
¼ cup flour
2 Tbsp. cooking oil

1 clove garlic, minced
2 large onions, sliced
1 Tbsp. Worcestershire sauce
2 8-oz. cans tomato sauce
1 dash red hot sauce

Trim fat edges from meat. Combine salt, pepper, flour. Divide in half and pound half of mixture into each side of steak. Heat oil in heavy frying pan and brown meat quickly on both sides. Add remaining ingredients, cover, reduce to simmer and cook about 2 hours or until meat is tender. If desired, thicken sauce before serving with meat. Serves 6.

Golden Onion Gravy for Steak

4 cups sliced onions
2 Tbsp. cooking oil
2 Tbsp. flour
2 cups meat stock

1 Tbsp. Worcestershire sauce
salt
freshly ground pepper

Heat oil in heavy frying pan and cook onions until light golden brown. Gradually stir in flour, stirring until smooth. Add remaining ingredients; reduce heat very low and cook until thick, stirring constantly. Cover and simmer 10 minutes. Serves 6.

Barbecued Short Ribs

Using 3 pounds beef short ribs, cut meat from bones into serving pieces. Marinate overnight in Southern Barbecue Sauce Supreme or your favorite sauce. Grill over hot charcoal, brushing often with barbecue sauce and turning to brown. Serves 6.

Southern Barbecue Sauce Supreme

1 lb. butter
1 pint apple cider vinegar
1 cup water
1 Tbsp. dry mustard
1 large onion, grated
5 Tbsp. Worcestershire sauce
2 cups tomato catsup

1 cup chili sauce
juice of 2 lemons
½ lemon, left whole, seeded
1 or 2 cloves garlic, chopped and tied
   in cheesecloth bag
2 tsp. sugar
1 bay leaf

Place all ingredients in saucepan and bring to a boil. Reduce to slow heat; simmer 30 minutes, stirring occasionally. Enough for 10 lbs. of beef, lamb or pork. Keep it warm and when meat on barbecue pit is ¾ done, swab with sauce frequently until done.

Spanish Beefburgers

1/2 cup finely chopped onions
1/4 cup chopped celery
1/4 cup chopped green pepper
3 Tbsp. melted butter
1 can condensed tomato soup

2 Tbsp. Worcestershire sauce
2 Tbsp. vinegar
1 Tbsp. prepared mustard
1 lb. ground beef, shaped into patties
bacon drippings

Cook onions, celery and green pepper in butter until onions are transparent. Add all remaining ingredients except beef; mix well and simmer 10 minutes stirring several times. In frying pan, brown beef patties in bacon drippings and cook until done. Place each patty on toasted roll, pour hot Spanish sauce over and serve hot. Serves 4 or 5.

Scrambled Hot Dogs

Kids love this one!

6 frankfurters, finely chopped
1/2 cup (2 oz.) shredded Cheddar cheese
1 Tbsp. chopped onion
2 Tbsp. chopped sweet pickle
3 Tbsp. catsup

1 tsp. prepared mustard
2 Tbsp. vegetable oil
1/2 tsp. salt
6 hot dog buns, split

Combine frankfurters, cheese, onion and pickle, stirring well. Mix together catsup, mustard, oil and salt; pour this mixture over frankfurter mixture and toss lightly. Spoon mixture into hot dog buns. Wrap each in aluminum foil and bake in 350°F oven for 20 minutes or until heated through. Makes 6 sandwiches.

MEXICAN RECIPES

Mexican Shrimp
Great appetizers!

24 large shrimp
1/2 cup lime juice
1/2 cup olive oil
5 cloves garlic, chopped

3 green chiles, peeled and chopped
    (or 1/2 tsp. cayenne pepper)
3 Tbsp. melted butter or margarine
minced parsley

Shell and devein shrimp, leaving tails intact. Marinate overnight in lime juice, oil and seasonings, using a glass or stainless steel dish. Heat broiler. Remove shrimp from marinade. Place in broiler pan and brush on butter or margarine. Broil until shrimp turns pink, about 5 minutes. Serve at once, sprinkled with minced parsley. Serves 4–6.

Grilled Catfish with Salsa

4 farm-raised catfish fillets or steaks
1/4 tsp. white pepper
1/2 teaspoon garlic salt

Salsa:
2 large, ripe tomatoes
1 clove garlic, peeled
3 green onions, chopped
1 4-oz. can green chiles, chopped
1 tsp. olive oil

1 Tbsp. lime juice
salt and pepper to taste
cilantro or parsley to taste (dried or
    chopped fresh)

Two hours before serving, combine peeled, seeded, quartered tomatoes with garlic, green onions and green chiles. Coarsely chop in food processor or blender. Stir in olive oil and lime juice. Add salt, pepper and cilantro to taste. Set aside to stand at least one hour for flavors to blend.

Sprinkle fillets with pepper and garlic salt. Place fillets in well-greased fish-grilling basket over hot coals. Grill 10 minutes per inch of thickness, turning once, until fish flakes easily. Serve hot with salsa. Serves 4. (Note: commercially prepared salsa may be substituted.)

Nifty Nachos

12 corn tortillas
peanut oil

1/2 lb. grated Longhorn cheese
1 can pickled jalapeño slices

Stack the tortillas on a cutting board and cut into 3 wedge-shaped pieces, for 36 pieces total. Heat 1/2 inch of peanut oil in a heavy skillet to 375°F. Fry 4 or 5 tortilla pieces in skillet at a time. Use a spatula to mash them down when they puff up; continue turning and mashing until they are flat, 60 seconds or less. Place cooked tortillas on a paper towel to drain. Drain oil from skillet.

Place crisp tortillas on a microwave-safe platter; cover with grated cheese and jalapeño slices. Microwave on high 1 1/2 to 3 1/2 minutes, until cheese melts. Serves 6–8. ✢

6 *Seminole Indians*

*The pride of the Seminole people, shown in this woman's face,
led them to fight for their right to Florida lands.*

Think of the Everglades and you think of Seminole Indians, yet they are not natives of Florida! When the Spanish first set foot in Florida they found some 10,000 Indians. Among them were the Calusas, fishermen and mariners in southwest Florida who violently opposed the white man's advance, and the Apalachee of the northwest, semi-civilized and powerful with a strong league of united chiefs.

After the English-Spanish struggle caused by the settling of Georgia and the Carolinas resulted in an English victory and James E. Oglethorpe founded Savannah in 1733, he swept south into Florida. A disastrous war had recently wiped out most of Florida's native Indians, and allies from the Lower Creek tribes came with Oglethorpe to help him fight. They liked the land and decided to stay.

Other Lower Creeks settled in the Apalachee region or moved into other north Florida areas. About 1775, their name became Seminole meaning runaway. By 1835, they were firmly settled.

The pride of the Seminole people led them to fight for their right to Florida lands and determined not to move. The seven towns they had in 1799 rapidly increased to 20 or more.

Hostilities with the U.S. began while the Spanish were still in control, especially during the War of 1812 and again in 1817–18, now called the first Seminole War. Gen. Andrew Jackson quelled the latter with 3,000 men—one reason for Spain ceding the territory to the U.S. in 1819.

By the St. Moultrie treaty in 1823, the Seminole ceded most of their lands except a central reservation. But pressure continued for their complete removal, so another treaty was negotiated at Payne's Landing in 1832, which compelled them to move west of the Mississippi within three years.

Most of the tribe, under Osceola's leadership, repudiated this last treaty, and so began the second war in 1835. It ended in August, 1842, and most of the tribe was moved west. But the cost was great—1,466 American lives and $20,000,000.

Some 300 Seminoles escaped into the watery wilderness of the Everglades, a slow-moving freshwater river 50 miles wide and a few inches deep, fed by Lake Okeechobee.

Until 1960, most Seminoles lived in "chickees"— a shelter without walls made with four poles, wooden floor and palm-thatched roof. Until millions of new residents cut severely into the hunting and fishing which was the food source for the tribe, the Indians lived a peaceable life among the animals and birds of the Everglades. They had three reservations, in Glades County, Broward County and Hendry County. However, in recent years they have found it necessary to organize under a Federal charter, become cattle ranchers and operators of a successful arts and crafts center and the Okalee Indian Village (open to tourists) on Dania plantation.

Approximately 300 are official members of the Seminole Tribe of Florida, but hundreds more live on six Florida reservations.

The Cow Creek Seminoles have learned to live and cooperate with the white man, although they have never accepted him. But the Mikasuki, many of whom live along Tamiami Trail and operate restaurants and tourist attractions, are more antagonistic and less prosperous.

The Seminoles have always been a proud race, self-reliant, tenacious of their opinions, true to the traditions of their race, with life based on matrilineal lineage. So a camp is usually composed of a woman, her daughters, and their children, and the husbands and unmarried brothers of these. When a man marries, he goes to his wife's camp, builds her a house and moves in.

Each household must contain the all-important sewing machine used to make the rainbow-colored, long-skirted costumes of the women and the shirts of the men. Young Seminoles now wear modern dress, but traditional costumes are still worn by elders of the tribe.

In their new homes, the Indians have electric ranges, but cooking is still done the old, primitive way deep in the reservations. The camp fire is unique. Several logs are arranged like spokes of a wheel, with the fire at the hub. Ends of the long logs extend into the fire and are continually pushed over the flame as it burns the wood.

Over this fire hangs a black iron pot filled with Soffkee, the standby food. This is a stew of meat, usually venison, with meal, grits and vegetables added. A wooden spoon is used and anyone may dip out a spoonful of stew when he feels hungry, any time of the day.

Their fruits are guavas, sour oranges and limes, bananas, wild berries and plums. In cleared land on the hummock, Seminoles grow corn, pumpkins, melons, sweet potatoes and sugar cane. Tender buds of the palmetto (called hearts of palm by the white man) are eaten year-round, raw or cooked.

When hunting is good, the men bag deer, quail, wild turkey, opossum, rabbit, squirrel; from Florida waters they take fish, turtles and oysters. When hunting is poor, they eat the chickens and pigs raised at home.

Coontie is the staff of life, the equivalent of our wheat bread. This wild cassava root grows only in south Florida and is called "God's gift to the Seminole." Very nutritious, it tastes something like arrowroot.

The Seminoles mash this root to pulp in mortars cut into cypress logs called coontie logs. The starch is then separated from the pulp with a straining cloth, yielding a yellowish-white flour used to bake their bright orange bread. At one time, coontie starch was used in food and for laundry and coontie-making was quite an industry in south Florida.

Several chiefs of the tribe have served as Baptist ministers, and many of the Indians have become Christians. Today, their aim is to enjoy modern living, give their children good educations, but never to surrender their revered Indian traditions.

Skillet Orange Duck

TIP: Rubbing a wild duck with lemon will help kill the gamey taste

1/3 cup all purpose flour	1 1/2 cups water
1 1/2 tsp. salt	1/3 cup cooking sherry
1/4 tsp. pepper	1/3 cup orange juice
3 ducks, quartered	2 Tbsp. orange marmalade
1/3 cup butter	1 Tbsp. grated orange rind

In bag, combine flour, salt, pepper. Shake duck in bag. Over medium heat in heavy iron skillet, brown duck in butter. Combine all remaining ingredients and pour over duck. Cover; simmer 1 1/2 hours or until tender. Serves 6.

Venison Soup

1 3-lb. venison roast	4 onions, cubed
4 cups cold water	1 clove garlic, chopped fine
1 Tbsp. salt	1 bay leaf
1 1/2 quarts water	1 Tbsp. parsley
1 bunch celery hearts, sliced	salt and pepper
2 cups tomatoes	flour
3 medium potatoes, cubed	

Soak roast in cold salt water overnight. Discard water and put meat in 1 1/2 quarts water. Simmer for 2 1/2 hours; remove and cool meat. Place in refrigerator overnight. Next day, skim off fat, simmer 2 hours; 20 minutes before meat is done, add celery, tomatoes, potatoes, onions, garlic, bay leaf. Add parsley and season to taste with salt and pepper. If necessary, thicken with a little flour. Serves 6–8.

Oyster-Cornbread Stuffing for Wild Turkey

6 Tbsp. butter	1 pint oysters with liquid
1/4 cup minced onion	3/4 tsp. salt
4 cups crumbled cornbread	1/4 tsp. paprika
2 lightly beaten eggs	2 Tbsp. minced parsley

Melt butter and saute onion until golden brown. Stir in all remaining ingredients. Toss lightly to mix. Cool before stuffing bird.

Fried Green Tomatoes

Use three mature, firm green tomatoes. Wash, dry and cut in thick slices. Sprinkle with salt, let stand 5 minutes then drain. Sprinkle with freshly ground black pepper. Dredge in corn meal and fry in hot oil until lightly browned. Serve hot. Serves 4.

Boiled Hardshell Crabs

Using 12 live hardshell crabs, plunge into boiling salted water in heavy large pot, cover and boil 15 to 20 minutes, or until red. Serve on heated platter with cracking tools and individual dishes of melted butter for each person. Crack shells and pick out the meat on underside of the shell and from the claws, also the tamale or green liver.

Corn Hoecake

Combine 2 cups white cornmeal with 1 teaspoon salt. Add enough boiling water (it must be boiling hot) to make a medium batter. Let stand for 1 hour. Heat bacon drippings in a heavy frying pan and place a heaping tablespoon full of batter in hot pan. Press down lightly with spatula to make cakes ½-inch thick. When one side is golden brown, turn and brown the other. Serve very hot. Especially good with turnip greens. Serves 6–8.

Roasting Ears

Using 4 ears unhusked fresh sweet corn, remove outer husks and silks. Leave inner husks on corn. In deep pot, submerge corn in 4 quarts of water with 6 tablespoons salt. Weight corn to hold it under water and soak 1 hour. Remove corn from water, place 1 teaspoon butter inside the ear on the kernels, wrap in aluminum foil and roast in 450°F oven about 25 minutes or until done. Serve hot with dish of melted butter, plenty of salt and pepper. Serves 4. (Note: Corn may also be roasted amid hot coals in barbecue pit—have coals well burned down with no flames—and cook about 10 minutes.)

Black-Eyed Peas with Dumplings

1 cup dried black-eyed peas	*1 tsp. salt*
3 cups water	*2 oz. salt pork or 1 Tbsp. cooking oil*

Dumplings:

2 cups flour	*1 tsp. salt*
4 tsp. baking powder	*about 1 cup milk*

Wash peas, cover with 3 cups water and soak overnight. Add salt and meat or oil to peas; bring to boil then reduce to simmer and cook covered until beans are tender; 15 minutes before end of cooking time, remove cover. Sift dry ingredients together, then add enough milk to make dough. If necessary, add enough water to peas to make about one cup liquid in pot. With fork and spoon, drop walnut-sized bits into peas, cover pot tightly; steam 15 minutes. Serves 4.

Using a unique four-log fire, a Seminole woman prepares pumpkin bread.

Baked Pumpkin Bread

The Seminoles use cooked, mashed pumpkin mixed with self-rising flour and water to make a soft dough They knead it in a ball until it is elastic then continue turning and folding until it is about ¼-inch thick. Small cakes are placed in a heavy iron skillet filled with smoking grease and fried until golden brown on each side. This makes a puffy, crisp bread.

This contemporary version of traditional bread is made with pumpkin but is baked in the oven!

1½ cups sifted flour	1 cup mashed pumpkin
1¼ tsp. baking soda	1 cup sugar
1 tsp. salt	½ cup buttermilk
1 tsp. ground cinnamon	1 egg, slightly beaten
½ tsp. ground nutmeg	2 Tbsp. soft butter

Sift together twice flour, baking soda, salt and spices. In large bowl, mix well pumpkin, sugar, buttermilk and slightly beaten egg. Stir in dry ingredients and butter. Beat at medium speed until blended. Turn into greased loaf pan and bake at 350°F for 1 hour.

Fried Frogs' Legs

Soak frogs' legs in equal amounts of salt water and milk for 1 hour. Drain; pat dry. Shake in bag of seasoned flour. Sauté in hot oil or butter until tender and brown. Serve with lemon or lime wedges.

Baked Rabbit

Skin and dress rabbit and cut into serving pieces. Shake in a bag of flour seasoned with salt and pepper. Fry in butter or bacon drippings until golden brown. Place in baking dish; cover with milk. Bake in 350°F oven about 1 hour or until tender. Mix a little flour with water and use to thicken milk for gravy. Pour over rabbit; serve hot. ✦

7 *Suwannee River Country*

*After Tallahassee was named territorial government seat,
lawmakers met in this three-story Capitol building.*

From Tallahassee to Gainesville, time has not touched the fairy tale beauty
of the gently rolling red clay hills, azure lakes and great live oaks trailing
Spanish moss. The Suwannee River meanders lazily across the state between
banks of lush green, shadowed by the spreading arms of ancient trees.

To the north and west, almost in the center of the panhandle, lies
Tallahassee, a Creek Indian word meaning "Old Town." The north Florida area
was first explored by Panfilo de Narvaez who landed at Tampa Bay in 1528. So
fierce was the Indian opposition to his march that only four men returned to
tell of the trip.

A year later, he was followed by Hernando de Soto who took his men
north into Georgia, fighting Indians all the way past an Indian village near the
modern city of Ocala, and into Tallahassee.

The city's first item of recorded history is dated 1539, when de Soto held a
powwow with the controlling Apalachee tribes, but this must have been a center for Indian activity long before that. De Soto wintered near Tallahassee with
a 600-man party, and it is believed that this marked the first observance of
Christmas in the New World.

In the 17th century, Spanish missions were strung out on the Suwannee and throughout north Florida from St. Augustine to the Gulf. One of these was the Spanish Mission of San Luis, established in 1633 near Tallahassee.

The Old World first learned of the beauty of the Suwannee River country with its springs and underground caverns when, just after the Revolutionary War in 1791, famous travel writer and botanist William Bartram published a book describing his Florida travels.

Titled *The Travels of William Bartram* and still in print, the book recreated the beauty of the region so well that it is believed by some scholars to have inspired many lines in Coleridge's poem, "Kubla Khan".

In 1812, Georgia settlers established a Republic of Florida. They were tormented by repeated Indian raids from tribes to the south until General Andrew Jackson swept down into Florida in 1814 to do battle. His victories weakened the hold of Spain on Florida cities, forcing the Spanish to sell Florida to the United States for five million dollars in 1819.

It was on March 4, 1824 that Tallahassee came into its own, when it was named the capital of the Territory of Florida.

During its first half century, the city saw rowdy backwoodsmen mingling on the streets with wealthy planters from Georgia, North Carolina and Virginia.

Social life was lively and festive, led by such celebrities as Prince Achille Murat, nephew of Napoleon Bonaparte. The Prince bought a large plantation near Tallahassee and married Catherine Willis, great-grandniece of George Washington, in Tallahassee. He recorded details of the elaborate dinner parties in his journal, writing, "No news in town except a wine party, or rather eating, drinking, card playing and see-gar smoking."

The burial place of the Prince and his lady is in the Episcopal Cemetery, one of the town sights.

The longest and costliest of America's Indian wars raged from 1833 to 1842, finally forcing the Seminoles to abandon their beloved hill country and flee south for safety into the Everglades.

The inflow of settlers increased and by 1845, there were many great plantations in north Florida raising cotton and sugar cane, producing cattle and hogs. The pretentious Maryland and Virginia late-Georgian Colonial mansions built then still stand, giving the area a genuine aura of the Old South.

Less elaborate but equally well proportioned are at least a dozen more mansions built in the 1830's in the antebellum towns of Madison, Monticello, Quincy and Marianna.

This has been retained because south Florida's boom skipped past this part of the state, so the old-time natural beauty remains largely intact. What began as a 15-home settlement is now a busy city with some 125,000 residents. But Tallahassee has not succumbed to the cosmopolitanism of a tourist state.

One still finds stately, white-columned homes furnished with rare antiques. Magnificent gardens are aflame with camellia, japonica and azalea each spring. Civil War trenches and breastworks adorn the town park. Downtown, a modern 22-story State Capitol has risen alongside the small 1902 Capitol building that offers visitors exhibits of Florida History.

Since 1857, Tallahassee has been the home of the Florida State University; since 1887, of the Florida Agricultural and Mechanical University.

In this placid land of magnolias and oleanders, the mint julep is popular and Southern food is still king. From nearby farmlands come garden vegetables, sweet potatoes, watermelons, pecans, corn, peanuts, Irish potatoes, sugar cane.

Game birds, homegrown beef, hogs and chickens are plentiful. Fried chicken, cornbread and biscuits, fruit puddings and pies, rich milk and cream desserts—these are among the homemade dishes still served with warm hospitality in north Florida homes.

Chicken Mousse

North Florida folk sometimes serve this with chilled watermelon rind pickles.

2 envelopes gelatin	*2 cups diced white chicken meat*
1/2 cup cold water	*1 cup diced celery*
1/2 cup boiling chicken stock	*1/2 cup mayonnaise*
1 cup cool stock	*1/2 cup heavy cream, whipped*
1 tsp. Worcestershire sauce	*1/2 cup grated almonds*
salt and pepper to taste	*2 tsp. chopped parsley*

Soften gelatin in cold water. Stir into hot stock until dissolved then combine with cool stock, Worcestershire sauce, salt and pepper. Refrigerate until consistency is like honey. Add all remaining ingredients. Turn into oiled mold. Chill till set then unmold and garnish with parsley. Serves 6.

Green Bean Salad

3 cups cooked green beans, drained
2 cups cooked green peas, drained
1/4 cup stuffed olives, sliced
1/4 cup almonds, sliced
2 cups celery, cut in 1/2-inch strips

1 cup green onions, sliced
2 cups raw carrots in 1/2-inch strips
1 bottle French salad dressing
2 slices bacon, cooked, drained and
   crumbled

Combine ingredients except bacon and marinate overnight in French dressing. Drain before serving. Crumble bacon over top just before serving. Serves 20.

Willie's Chicken Dressing

Guests frequently skip the chicken to save room for this superb dressing.

chicken giblets
1 tsp. salt
4 peppercorns
1 onion, stuck with 4 cloves
1 carrot, scraped
3 cups crumbled cornbread

3 cups crumbled biscuits
1 tsp. salt
1 tsp. poultry seasoning
2 medium onions, chopped fine
3 celery stalks, chopped fine
1 cup pecans, chopped fine

The night before, place chicken giblets in one quart of salted water with peppercorns, onion and carrot; bring to a boil and reduce heat to simmer to make chicken stock. Set aside giblets to use in gravy. Mix together all ingredients; add enough stock to moisten. Pack into square, greased baking pan and bake in 350°F oven until brown, 25–30 minutes. Dressing may also be used to stuff the bird instead of being baked separately. Serves 6–8.

Chicken Giblet Gravy

chicken giblets and neck
1 tsp. salt
4 peppercorns
1 onion, stuck with 4 cloves

1 carrot, scraped
3 Tbsp. flour
1 hard-cooked egg, chopped
salt and pepper

If giblets have not been cooked (as in above recipe), place giblets in one quart of water with salt, peppercorns, onion, carrot; bring to boil then reduce heat to simmer. Cook until tender. Chop giblets and neck meat and set aside. Strain broth, discarding vegetables. Remove chicken from roasting pan; pour out all but 3 tablespoons drippings. Over low heat, blend in flour, stirring constantly. Pour 1 cup giblet broth into roasting pan and stir until brown bits are loose. Add remaining 1 cup of broth and stir until gravy is very smooth and hot. Add chopped giblets and chopped, hard-cooked egg. Correct seasoning. Makes 2 cups.

Florida French Dressing

1/3 cup orange juice
1 cup salad oil
1/4 cup vinegar
1/2 tsp. Worcestershire sauce
1/2 tsp. paprika

1 small clove garlic, minced
2 Tbsp. lemon juice
1/3 cup confectioners' sugar
1/2 tsp. salt
1/4 tsp. dry mustard

Mix all together and shake in jar until blended. Makes 1½ cups.

Southern Mashed Potato Salad

8 to 10 medium potatoes
1½ tsp. salt
1/4 tsp. pepper
1/4 cup cider vinegar
1¼ cups mayonnaise

6 hard-cooked eggs, chopped
1 small jar pimientos, chopped
1/2 cup chopped green onion tops
3/4 cup chopped green pepper
1 cup chopped celery

Boil potatoes in salted water, covered, until tender. Drain well. In pot, mash until smooth. Stir in thoroughly salt, pepper, vinegar and mayonnaise. Add eggs and all other ingredients; toss gently. Pack into ring mold, turn out and serve while warm. May also be chilled and garnished with parsley or raw vegetables. Serves 10.

Crisp Green Tomato Pickles

4 quarts thinly sliced green tomatoes
1 quart thinly sliced white onions
1/3 cup salt
3 cups white vinegar
1 tsp. whole allspice
2 tsp. whole black pepper

1 Tbsp. celery seed
2 Tbsp. white mustard seed
1 lemon, thinly sliced
2 drops red hot sauce
3 cups packed brown sugar

Sprinkle 1/3 cup salt on tomatoes and onion; leave overnight, covered. Drain. Place all remaining ingredients in pot; bring to boil and add tomatoes and onion. Bring to boil then reduce to simmer and cook about 10 minutes, stirring several times. Pour into hot sterilized jars and seal. Makes 5 pints.

Honey Fruit Salad Dressing

1 cup heavy cream, whipped
3 Tbsp. honey

1 Tbsp. lime or lemon juice
1/8 tsp. ground mace

Beat cream just until stiff then beat in remaining ingredients. Use as dessert sauce over fresh or canned peaches, pineapple, pears, or other fruit.

Sunshine Chicken Salad

1¹/2 cups cooked diced chicken
³/4 cup diced celery
¹/2 cup white grapes, halved
¹/2 cup Creamy Fruit Dressing (below)

salad greens
¹/2 avocado, sliced
¹/4 cup chopped pecans
6 canned spiced crabapples

Add Creamy Fruit Dressing to chicken, celery and grapes. Place greens on plates with salad in center. Sprinkle with chopped pecans; garnish with sliced avocado and crabapples. Serves 6.

Creamy Fruit Dressing:
2 tsp. salt
1 tsp. sugar
¹/2 tsp. paprika

¹/2 cup lemon juice
1¹/2 cups salad oil
1¹/3 cups heavy cream

In a jar, shake together all ingredients except cream. Gradually add the cream, beating with a rotary beater until thick. Makes 3¹/3 cups; recipe may be cut halved, to make about 1³/4 cups.

Roast Pork with Tropical, Five-Fruit Glaze

3-lb. boneless pork loin, trimmed of most fat and tied

For Glaze:
3 Tbsp. butter or margarine
3 Tbsp. apricot preserves
3 Tbsp. currant jelly
3 Tbsp. guava paste or jelly

1 Tbsp. lemon juice
2 Tbsp. Dijon mustard
2 Tbsp. orange liqueur (Triple Sec or
    Cointreau)

Spray roasting rack with vegetable oil and place in roasting pan lined with aluminum foil. Place roast in pan, fat side up; set aside. Make glaze by combining butter, preserves, jellies, lemon juice and mustard in saucepan. Simmer until butter melts; add liqueur and cook 3 minutes more. Brush over pork roast.

Bake pork roast uncovered in 350°F oven 1¹/2 to 2 hours, or until meat thermometer reads 170°F. During last 30 minutes of cooking time, baste several times with glaze mixture. Remove cooked roast from oven; let set 15 minutes before carving. Serves 6.

Mock Oysters

1 cup corn cut from cob (or frozen)
1 Tbsp. butter, melted
2 egg yolks, separated
1/2 tsp. salt
1/8 tsp. ground black pepper

dash cayenne
1/4 tsp. ground thyme
1/2 cup sifted all-purpose flour
cooking oil
celery salt

Combine corn, butter, egg yolks, seasoning and flour. Beat egg whites until they stand in soft, stiff peaks and fold into mixture. Drop from teaspoon into deep cooking oil, preheated to 350°F. Fry until golden. Drain on paper towels. Sprinkle lightly with celery salt. Serve as appetizers. Makes 60.

Glorified Summer Squash

2 cups cooked yellow squash
3/4 cup bread crumbs
3 Tbsp. butter
1/2 cup milk
2 Tbsp. chopped onion
2 Tbsp. chopped green pepper
1 Tbsp. chopped pimiento

2 Tbsp. tomato catsup
salt, pepper to taste
3/4 cup grated Cheddar cheese
2 beaten eggs
1 cup buttered bread crumbs
paprika

Boil squash in salted water until tender. Mash fine; add all other ingredients, except bread crumbs and paprika. Pour into buttered baking dish. Top with buttered bread crumbs; sprinkle with paprika. Bake in 350°F oven until firm 25 to 30 minutes. Serves 4–6.

Old South Tomato Salad

3 medium tomatoes, sliced
1 onion cut into rings
salad greens
1/3 cup French salad dressing
3/4 tsp. celery seed

1/4 cup pickle relish
6 slices crisp cooked bacon, crumbled
2 hard-cooked eggs, quartered
monosodium glutamate

Arrange tomatoes and onion rings on crisp greens. Blend French dressing with celery seed and pickle relish; pour over tomatoes and onions. Sprinkle with monosodium glutamate; scatter bacon on top and garnish with eggs. Serves 6.

Southern Corn Pudding

3 eggs
2 cups cream style canned corn
2 Tbsp. melted butter
2 cups scalded milk
2 tsp. salt

dash pepper
2 Tbsp. flour
1 Tbsp. sugar
cracker crumbs
butter

Beat eggs well. Combine with all ingredients. Pour into buttered casserole. Sprinkle with crumbs; dot with butter. Place in pan of warm water. Bake in 325°F oven, uncovered, 1 hour 15 minutes. Serves 6.

Deviled Fresh Carrots

12 young tender carrots
1/2 cup butter or margarine
2 Tbsp. light brown sugar
3/4 tsp. salt

1 tsp. dry mustard
1/8 tsp. ground black pepper
dash cayenne pepper

Wash carrots, peel and cut each in half lengthwise. Saute in butter 5 minutes. Add salt and spices. Cover and cook 10 minutes or until carrots are tender. Serve hot. Serves 6.

Buttermilk Biscuits

2 cups flour
2 tsp. baking powder
1/4 tsp. soda

1 tsp. salt
1 cup buttermilk
2 Tbsp. lard or ham fat

Measure 2 heaping tablespoons of flour and use to flour surface. Put remaining flour in bowl, make a hole in center of flour and put into this the baking powder, baking soda and salt. Add shortening; pour in buttermilk. With finger tips, gradually mix, using enough milk to make a soft dough. Turn onto floured surface and pat gently to 1/2 inch thickness. Cut out with biscuit cutter and place in greased pan. Bake at 400°F until brown on bottom (about 15 minutes) then place under broiler for a minute or two, if necessary to brown tops. Makes about 20 biscuits.

Pecan Waffles

2 cups sifted all-purpose flour
1 tsp. baking soda
1 Tbsp. sugar
1/2 tsp. salt
2 eggs, separated

1/4 cup vinegar
13/4 cups sweet milk
1/3 cup melted shortening
3/4 cup chopped pecans

Sift together flour, baking soda, sugar and salt. Beat together egg yolks, vinegar, milk then mix with dry ingredients. Stir in melted shortening and pecans, stirring until smooth. Use mixer to beat egg whites till stiff but not dry; fold into batter. Pour on heated waffle iron; bake until steaming stops. Serve with warm syrup and butter. Serves 4.

Honey-Pecan Banana Bread

11/4 cups shortening
2 cups sugar
4 eggs
1 cup honey
21/2 cups mashed ripe bananas

5 cups sifted all-purpose flour
21/2 tsp. baking powder
21/2 tsp. baking soda
1 tsp. salt
2 cups chopped pecans

Cream shortening and sugar. Add eggs one at a time while creaming. Add honey and bananas; mix thoroughly. Sift flour, baking powder, soda and salt together. Add to batter, mixing well. Fold in chopped pecans. Pour batter into three 4- x 8- x 21/2-inch loaf pans, lightly greased on bottom and sides, filling each slightly more than 3/4 full. Bake in 350°F oven 45 to 55 minutes or until tester comes out clean. Makes 3 loaves.

Honey Pecan Pie

single 9-inch pie crust
3 eggs
1/3 cup granulated sugar
1/3 cup light brown sugar
1/4 tsp. salt

1/4 cup melted butter
1/2 cup honey
1/2 cup white corn syrup
1 tsp. vanilla
1 cup pecan halves

Beat eggs. Mix in all other ingredients except pecan halves; pour into pastry-lined 9-inch pie pan Arrange pecan halves on filling in desired pattern Bake 40 to 50 minutes at 375°F until set and pastry is golden. Cool. Serve cold or slightly warm.

Through the window drifts the rich aroma of Yam Praline Pie.

Yam Praline Pie

2 eggs
1/2 cup granulated sugar
1/2 cup packed light brown sugar
1 tsp. cinnamon
1/2 tsp. nutmeg
1/2 tsp. ginger

1/4 tsp. salt
2 cups cooked, mashed fresh yams
3/4 cup milk
1 cup light cream
1 unbaked 9-inch pastry shell
1/3 cup chopped pecans

Praline Topping:
1/3 cup chopped pecans
1/2 cup packed brown sugar
3 Tbsp. softened butter

Beat eggs in mixing bowl; beat in granulated and brown sugars, spices and salt. Blend in yams. Gradually stir in milk and cream. Pour into unbaked pastry shell. Bake in 400°F oven 10 minutes. Reduce heat to 350°F and bake 20 minutes. Combine topping ingredients; sprinkle over surface of pie. Continue baking 25 minutes until knife inserted near center comes out dean. Cool completely before serving.

Creole Sweet Potato-Pecan Pie

9-inch unbaked pie shell
1/3 cup granulated white sugar
1/3 cup light brown sugar
1/4 tsp. salt
3/4 tsp. ground ginger
3/4 tsp. ground cinnamon
1/2 tsp. ground nutmeg
1/16 tsp. ground cloves

1 cup mashed sweet potatoes
2 well beaten eggs
3/4 cup hot milk
1/2 cup light brown sugar
1/4 cup (1/2 stick) butter or margarine, softened
1/4 cup pecans, chopped medium fine

Line 9-inch pie plate with unbaked pastry; set aside. Combine white and brown sugars, salt and spices in mixing bowl. Blend in mashed sweet potatoes. Beat in eggs. Stir in hot milk. Pour into unbaked pie shell. Bake 25 minutes in preheated 375°F oven. Meanwhile, blend 1/2 cup brown sugar with butter or margarine and pecans. Sprinkle over partially baked pie. Continue baking 30 minutes or until filling is firm in center. Serve cold with whipped cream. ✻

8 Florida Panhandle

*Steep steps climb the crumbling brick wall of
Fort San Carlos, built in Fernandina after 1784.*

History was made in Pensacola, the second oldest city in the United States. In four centuries, the people have lived under 17 changes of government, and five flags: Spanish, French, British, Confederate, and American.

The first colony was founded when Tristan de Luna landed in Pensacola Bay with 1500 persons in 1559, but a hurricane hit the fleet and the venture ended in just two years. Today, a cross in the sand is a reminder of the event.

After establishing St. Augustine, the Spanish returned to Pensacola in 1698 to build a fort. The French moved down the Mississippi and took the fort in 1719 but lost it again to the Spanish, and so it went.

After Great Britain ceded Florida to Spain in 1783, there were frequent Indian raids and Andrew Jackson waged successful attacks in Florida, then set up a military government in 1818. In 1821, he became provisional governor when Spain gave Florida up to the U. S., and Pensacola was his headquarters.

Important because it is the state's largest natural deep-water harbor, Pensacola had a U.S. Navy Yard built in 1825 and has remained an important military bastion ever since. Fort Pickens on Santa Rosa Island was a key Union stronghold during the War Between the States, when Union forces held the fort and imprisoned Geronimo and his Apaches.

Inside famous Pensacola Naval Air Station, where naval aviation was born, are Forts San Carlos, Barrancas and Redoubt.

The Confederates were ordered to abandon the city in February, 1862; supplies and troops were moved out. Most citizens left, burning what they could not carry, and by May, Federal troops took over. There was a long listless period followed by the Reconstruction, then the timber and naval stores in the area began moving out on new railroads.

The waterfront was improved during the busy 1870's, berthing ships from Italy and France, from England and Sweden. A disastrous fire swept the town in 1880, but by 1900, Pensacola was the second largest city in Florida with 18,000 residents.

The Government built its first training base for naval aviators there in 1914. This is one of the events recorded in the history of Naval aviation from its beginnings to the space age, which is shown in the Naval Air Museum at the Naval Air Station.

This quiet city is thriving, but life continues at a pleasant, leisurely pace. Summers, this westernmost section of Florida is filled with Southern tourists flocking to the magnificent beaches of Santa Rosa Island, part of a great state park which offers swimming, fishing and boating. The beaches are famous for their long stretches of pure white sand.

Hunting for quail, turkey and deer is done in Apalachicola National Forest, which spreads over 600,000 acres and is the largest of the state's three national forests. And for fishing buffs, there is fun to be had angling for fine specimens of red snapper, tarpon, channel bass, sea trout, mackerel, amberjack, grouper, and more, from old Pensacola Bay Bridge—"the world's longest fishing pier."

Pensacola itself is more Spanish than American and the wrought iron decorating the houses is a tipoff that, historically and architecturally, the town is more closely related to New Orleans and Mobile than to Florida cities. Old balconies, graceful gables and wrought-iron balustrades contribute to the romantic, Old World atmosphere along oak-shaded streets.

Pensacola has a proud group of "Creoles" with a combined African-Spanish heritage, as well as a prosperous African-American population. Traditional cooking of the Old South blends with all the varied nationalities to create a unique cuisine.

It's an old Pensacola custom to have a "hospitality table" near the front door of each home at Christmas time, laden with fruit and homemade goodies.

Southern foods take on added Spanish and Creole spiciness in the steaming seafood chowders, crusty brown barbecued chicken and fish, Gaspachee (better known as Gazpacho) salad, homemade mincement, baked grits, Hoppin' John, and much more.

In magnolia-shaded Pensacola, and in other Florida cities along the Gulf Coast—Fort Walton Beach, Panama City, Apalachicola—the unique handling of fresh seafood is superb, not to be missed!

PANHANDLE SPECIALTIES

Deviled Crabs

1 lb. crabmeat
1 cup cracker crumbs
3 eggs, lightly beaten
1/2 cup finely minced celery
1/2 cup minced green pepper
2 Tbsp. lemon juice
1 Tbsp. vinegar

1 Tbsp. Worcestershire sauce
1/2 tsp. salt
1/2 tsp. black pepper
few drops Tabasco
1 cup melted butter
8 crab shells

Beat eggs lightly Mix all ingredients lightly. Stuff into 8 crab shells. Bake at 375°F for about 12 minutes, until piping hot. Serves 8.

Pickled Shrimp

1 cup salad oil
1 cup white vinegar
juice of 1/2 lemon
1 tsp. dill seed
1 tsp. peppercorns

1 stick cinnamon
1 tsp. cloves
1 tsp. salt
1 onion. sliced
2 lbs. cleaned, boiled shrimp

Cook together for 10 minutes first 8 ingredients. Cool. Slice onion and place in bowl with cold shrimp. Pour pickling mixture over shrimp; refrigerate overnight. (Keeps well up to a week.) Drain; serve as appetizer, or on a salad plate.

Oysters Pensacola

1/4 cup grated onion
1/4 cup finely chopped parsley
3 Tbsp. finely chopped celery
1 tsp. lemon juice
1/4 tsp. salt

1/8 tsp. pepper
few drops Tabasco
1/2 cup butter
3 dozen oysters on the half shell
buttered crumbs

Cream butter then add onion, parsley, celery, lemon juice and seasonings. Place oysters on half shell in shallow baking pan. Top each with a spoonful of the onion and butter mixture. Sprinkle with buttered crumbs and bake in 375°F oven about 30 minutes, until crumbs are brown. Serves 6.

From Florida waters, a platter of succulent Oysters Pensacola.

Snapper Red and Green

1–1½ lb. red snapper fillets or steaks
2 tsp. lime juice
1 onion, chopped
1 green pepper, cut into
   1- x ¼-inch strips
2 cloves garlic, minced

2 Tbsp. olive oil
2 14-oz. cans whole, peeled tomatoes
⅛ tsp. ground red pepper (or to taste)
½ cup sliced green olives,
   pimiento-stuffed

Sprinkle snapper with lime juice and set aside at room temperature while preparing sauce. In large skillet over medium high heat, saute onion, green pepper and garlic in oil until onion is tender. Add tomatoes and liquid and red pepper. Cook 5 minutes, stirring occasionally. Arrange fillets over sauce; scatter olives over fish. Reduce heat to low. Cook, covered, until fish flakes with a fork (allow 10 minutes for each inch of fillets, measured at thickest place). Serve snapper hot with sauce, adding more olives if desired. Serves 2.

Baked Grits

1 cup milk	2 eggs beaten until frothy
2 Tbsp. butter	1/2 tsp. salt
2 cups cooked grits	dash of pepper

Heat milk and butter. Add and mix until smooth the grits, eggs, salt and pepper. Pour into buttered casserole and bake at 325°F until firm and golden brown, about 35 minutes. Serves 4–6.

Gaspachee (Pensacola Salad)

The hardtack made today is not as rock hard as that of early times, so it needs only a brief soaking. (If hardtack is not available in your area, you can order it from Premier Bakery, 1124 West Garden Street, Pensacola, 32501.)

2 hardtack or pilot bread	1 medium onion, chopped
2 chopped cucumbers	4 chopped stalks of celery
2 chopped large ripe tomatoes	about 3/4 cup mayonnaise
1 chopped green pepper	salt, pepper to taste

Soak hardtack in water for about ten minutes. Squeeze dry of all water; add vegetable ingredients, mayonnaise, salt and pepper. (Be sure the vegetables are very finely chopped and well chilled, for best flavor.)

Southern Spoon Bread

Every Florida pioneer has a favorite recipe!

4 cups milk	1 1/2 tsp. salt
1 cup white corn meal	1 tsp. double-acting baking powder
2 Tbsp. butter	4 well-beaten eggs

Over hot water in double boiler, scald milk; gradually add corn meal and continue to cook and stir until thick. Add butter, salt, and baking powder; mix well. Then add hot mixture slowly to beaten eggs, stirring constantly. Pour into greased 2-quart casserole. Bake in 425°F oven 45 minutes or until set. Serve at once in baking dish with plenty of butter. Serves 8.

Shrimp Creole

¹/₂ lb. salt pork
2 medium onions, chopped
1 medium green pepper, chopped
2 celery stalks, chopped
2 15-oz. cans tomatoes

1 10¹/₄-oz. can tomato soup
1 4-oz. can tomato paste
salt, pepper, Worcestershire to taste
3 lbs. shrimp
2 cups uncooked rice

Dice salt pork and fry until crisp and brown in heavy skillet. Remove bacon from pan, leaving all melted drippings in skillet. Add chopped onions, pepper, and celery to pan drippings; simmer until soft. Add tomatoes, soup, tomato paste. Season to taste with salt, pepper, Worcestershire. Cook on low heat until thick, about 2 hours, stirring occasionally.

While sauce is cooking, prepare shrimp. Rinse well under cool, running water. Cook in large pot containing 3 or more quarts of boiling, salted water 10 to 12 minutes, just until shells turn pink. Remove from heat, cool in cooking water about 20 minutes, drain. When cool, remove shells and devein. Add shrimp to cooked sauce, saving 6–8 large shrimp to garnish top. Cook rice according to package directions; cover with Shrimp Creole and garnish. Serves 8.

Hoppin' John

2 cups blackeyed peas
¹/₄ lb. lean salt pork, sliced
2 cups cooked rice

salt and pepper to taste
dash of Tabasco

Wash peas and soak overnight. Drain. Add sliced salt pork. Cover with salted water and cook about 40 minutes, or until tender. Some liquid should remain in the pan; if not, add enough to cover bottom of pan. Stir in cooked rice and seasonings. Place over low heat and stir; cover and heat. Serve immediately. Serves 4–6.

"PEANUTTY" RECIPES

Baked Apples with Peanut Topping

4 medium apples	1/4 cup sugar
1/3 cup raisins	1/2 tsp. cinnamon
1/2 cup orange juice	1 tsp. grated orange rind
1/2 cup water	1 1/2 Tbsp. butter
2 Tbsp. flour	1 1/2 Tbsp. peanut butter
1/8 tsp. salt	1/4 cup chopped salted peanuts

Core apples without cutting through the blossom end. Pare apples one third of way down. Put raisins into centers of apples. Place apples in a baking dish and pour orange juice and water around them. Combine flour, salt, sugar, cinnamon, orange rind, butter and peanut butter, mixing until crumbly. Stir in peanuts. Spoon mixture over apples, piling some in a mound on top. Bake at 375°F about 1 hour, basting with the liquid every 15 minutes. The top of the filling may be toasted by placing in the broiler the last 5 minutes. Serves 4.

Peanut Butter Sauce for Vegetables

1 Tbsp. butter or margarine	1/2 tsp. salt
1/4 cup peanut butter	pepper
2 tsp. flour	1 cup milk

Melt butter in pan over boiling water. Blend in the peanut butter. Add flour and seasonings and stir until smooth. Stir in milk slowly. Cook over boiling water until thick, stirring constantly. Serve on cooked cabbage, onions or cauliflower. Makes about 1 cup.

Creamed Celery with Peanuts

1 1/2 cups celery cut in 1-inch pieces	pepper
3/4 cup liquid (cooking liquid plus milk)	1 Tbsp. butter or margarine
1 Tbsp. flour	1/4 cup grated cheese
1/4 tsp. salt	1/4 cup chopped salted peanuts

Cook celery until tender in small amount of boiling salted water. Drain, retaining liquid. Measure cooking liquid and add enough milk to make 3/4 cup. Mix flour and part of liquid until smooth. Stir into rest of liquid. Add seasonings and butter; cook slowly until sauce thickens, stirring frequently. Stir celery and cheese into the sauce. As soon as cheese melts, remove from heat. Add peanuts. Serves 4.

Peanut Butter Muffins

2 cups sifted flour
3 tsp. baking powder
1 tsp. salt
¼ cup sugar

⅓ cup peanut butter
2 eggs, beaten
1 cup milk
2 Tbsp. melted butter or margarine

Sift dry ingredients together. Work in peanut butter. Combine eggs and milk; pour into dry ingredients. Add butter and stir just enough to moisten dry ingredients. Fill greased muffin pans ⅔ full and bake in 400°F oven 25 minutes. Makes 12 large muffins. ✦

Index

SALADS & DRESSINGS (continued):
Florida French Dressing 85
Fruit Salad with Orange Cream
Salad Dressing 62
Gaspachee 96
Grapefruit Cole Slaw 62
Grapefruit-Avocado Salad 62
Green Bean Salad 84
Honey Fruit Salad Dressing 85
JFK Salad Dressing 24
Lime French Dressing 27
Lime Sour 44
Louis Pappas' Greek Salad 52
Old South Tomato Salad 87
Prize-Winning Shrimp-Stuffed
Avocados 28
Red-and-White Tomato
Molded Salad 14
Southern Mashed Potato Salad 85
Sunshine Chicken Salad 86

SAUCES & GRAVIES
Chicken Giblet Gravy 84
Golden Onion Gravy for Steak 70
Peanut Butter Sauce for
Vegetables 98
Southern Barbecue
Sauce Supreme 70

SOUPS
Conch Chowder 37
Ocean Reef Grouper Chowder 39
Pompano Stew 39
Cream of Avocado Soup 28
Spanish Bean Soup 50
Venison Soup 77

VEGETABLES & SIDE DISHES
Baked Grits 96
Black-Eyed Peas with Dumplings 78
Broccoli Soufflé with
Cheese Sauce 14
Corn Fritters 60
Corn Hoecake 78
Creamed Celery with Peanuts 98
Cuban Black Beans 21
Deviled Fresh Carrots 88
Fried Green Tomatoes 77
Frijoles Negros a la Cubana 21
Glorified Summer Squash 87
Green Banana Puree 22
Green Bean Salad 84
Hoppin' John 97
Hot Bollos (Spanish Appetizers) 15
Mock Oysters 87
Orange Sweet Potato Cups 62
Oyster-Cornbread Stuffing for
Wild Turkey 77
Potato Pancakes (Latkes) 25
Roasting Ears 78
Southern Corn Pudding 15, 88
Southern Mashed Potato Salad 85
Southern Spoon Bread 96
Willie's Chicken Dressing 84

WILD GAME
Baked Rabbit 80
Fried Frog Legs 80
Oyster-Cornbread Stuffing for
Wild Turkey 77
Skillet Orange Duck 77
Venison Soup 77

Notes